Computer Graphics with OpenGL

A Comprehensive Guide to Real-Time 3D Graphics

James R. Bromley

Copyright © 2024 by James R. Bromley

No part of this publication may be reproduced, distributed, or transmitted in any form or by any means, including photocopying, recording, or other electronic or mechanical methods, without the prior written permission of the publisher, except in the case of brief quotations embodied in critical reviews and certain other noncommercial uses permitted by copyright law.

Disclaimer

This book is intended to provide general information and is not a substitute for legal, professional, or expert advice. While every effort has been made to ensure accuracy, the author and publisher assume no responsibility for errors or omissions. The views expressed in this book are solely those of the author and do not necessarily reflect the views of any organization or institution.

Contents

Part 1: Foundations 4

1. Introduction to Computer Graphics and OpenGL 5
   1.1 What is Computer Graphics? 5
   1.2 History of OpenGL 7
   1.3 OpenGL's Role in Modern Graphics 8
   1.4 Setting Up Your Development Environment 10
   1.5 Basic OpenGL Concepts: Vertices, Primitives, and Pipelines 12
   1.6 Your First OpenGL Program: A Simple Triangle 15

2. OpenGL Fundamentals 20
   2.1 Window Creation and Context Management 20
   2.2 Shaders: Vertex and Fragment Shaders 23
   2.3 Data Buffers: Vertex Buffer Objects (VBOs) 27
   2.4 Index Buffers: Element Buffer Objects (EBOs) 30
   2.5 Transformations: Translation, Rotation, Scaling 33
   2.6 Matrices: Model, View, and Projection Matrices 37

3. Lighting and Materials 40
   3.1 Light Sources: Ambient, Diffuse, Specular 40
   3.2 Materials: Properties and Lighting Models 42
   3.3 Phong Shading and Blinn-Phong Shading 44
   3.4 Lighting Techniques: Directional, Point, and Spot Lights 46

Part 2: Advanced Techniques 49

4. Textures and Sampling 50
   4.1 Texture Mapping: 2D, 3D, and Cube Maps 50
   4.2 Texture Filtering: Mipmapping and Anisotropic Filtering 53
   4.3 Texture Coordinates and Sampling 56
   4.4 Texture Blending and Operations 58

5. Geometry Shaders and Tessellation 61
   5.1 Geometry Shader Concepts and Applications 61
   5.2 Tessellation Control and Evaluation Shaders 63
   5.3 Creating Tessellated Surfaces: Patches and Levels of Detail 66

6. Framebuffers and Render Targets 70
   6.1 Framebuffer Objects (FBOs): Creating and Using 70
   6.2 Render-to-Texture (RTT): Rendering to Textures 74
   6.3 Depth and Stencil Buffers: Advanced Rendering Techniques 76

Part 3: Real-World Applications 79

7. 3D Modeling and Scene Graphs 80

    7.1 Loading and Rendering 3D Models..80
    7.2 Scene Graphs: Organizing and Managing 3D Scenes.......................83
    7.3 Model Transformation and Animation.. 86

8. Game Development with OpenGL.. 90
    8.1 Game Loop and Input Handling.. 90
    8.2 Collision Detection and Response.. 93
    8.3 Character and Object Animation.. 95
    8.4 Game Physics and Dynamics... 97

9. OpenGL and Other Technologies.. 100
    9.1 Integrating OpenGL with Other APIs (e.g., DirectX, Vulkan)............100
    9.2 OpenGL and Virtual Reality (VR)... 102
    9.3 OpenGL and Augmented Reality (AR)... 105

Part 4: Best Practices and Optimization... 108

10. OpenGL Debugging and Profiling.. 109
    10.1 Debugging Techniques: Using OpenGL's Debug Output............... 109
    10.2 Profiling Performance: Identifying Bottlenecks.............................. 113
    10.3 Optimization Strategies: Reducing Overdraw and Improving Efficiency... 115

11. Cross-Platform Development with OpenGL..119
    Cross-Platform Development Frameworks for OpenGL.......................122

12. The Future of OpenGL: Latest Versions and Extensions.................126
    12.1 Latest OpenGL Versions and Extensions....................................... 126
    12.2 Trends in Real-Time 3D Graphics.. 128

Appendix... 131
    A: OpenGL Mathematics... 131
    B: GLSL Syntax and Built-in Functions... 133

Part 1: Foundations

1. Introduction to Computer Graphics and OpenGL

1.1 What is Computer Graphics?

Computer Graphics is the field of study and practice that deals with the creation and manipulation of images and visual content using computers. It encompasses a wide range of techniques and applications, from simple 2D drawings to complex 3D animations and interactive simulations.

Key Aspects of Computer Graphics:

- **Image Synthesis:**
    - Generating images from scratch, often based on mathematical models or algorithms.
    - This includes techniques like ray tracing, rasterization, and procedural generation.
- **Image Processing:**
    - Manipulating existing images, such as enhancing, filtering, and transforming them.
    - This involves techniques like image editing, color correction, and image recognition.
- **Computer Animation:**
    - Creating the illusion of motion by rapidly displaying a sequence of still images.
    - This includes techniques like keyframing, motion capture, and physics-based animation.
- **User Interfaces:**

- Designing and implementing visual interfaces for computer systems.
- This includes elements like windows, icons, menus, and 3D user interfaces.
- **Visualization:**
  - Representing data and information visually, such as scientific visualizations, medical imaging, and data dashboards.

Applications of Computer Graphics:

Computer Graphics has a profound impact on various fields:

- **Entertainment:** Movies, video games, television shows, and virtual reality experiences.
- **Design:** Industrial design, architectural visualization, and fashion design.
- **Medicine:** Medical imaging, surgical simulations, and prosthetics design.
- **Science and Engineering:** Scientific visualization, simulations, and data analysis.
- **Business:** Marketing, advertising, and e-commerce.

Key Concepts in Computer Graphics:

- **Pixels:** The smallest unit of a digital image.
- **Resolution:** The number of pixels in an image, determining its sharpness and detail.
- **Color Models:** Systems for representing colors, such as RGB, CMYK, and HSV.
- **Geometric Primitives:** Basic shapes like points, lines, polygons, and curves.
- **Transformations:** Operations that change the position, size, or orientation of objects.

1.2 History of OpenGL

OpenGL (Open Graphics Library) has a rich history, evolving alongside the advancements in computer graphics hardware and software.

- **Birth at Silicon Graphics (SGI)**: OpenGL was born in 1991 at Silicon Graphics, Inc. (SGI), a pioneer in computer graphics workstations. SGI recognized the need for a standardized, platform-independent API for 3D graphics programming.
- **The First Release: OpenGL 1.0** : In 1992, OpenGL 1.0 was released, marking a significant milestone. It provided a set of functions for rendering 3D graphics primitives like points, lines, and polygons.
- **Khronos Group Takes Over** : In 2006, OpenGL was handed over to the Khronos Group, a consortium of companies working to create open standards for the acceleration of multimedia.
- **Evolution and Advancements** : Over the years, OpenGL has undergone numerous revisions and improvements. Key milestones include:
    - **OpenGL 2.0** (2004): Introduced programmable shaders, giving developers more control over the rendering pipeline.
    - **OpenGL 3.0** (2008): Focused on a more modern, core profile, removing deprecated functionality.
    - **OpenGL 4.x** : Continued to add features like tessellation shaders, geometry shaders, and support for newer hardware capabilities.

OpenGL's Impact:

- **Platform Independence** : OpenGL's cross-platform nature has been a key factor in its success, allowing developers to write graphics applications that can run on various operating systems and hardware.
- **Industry Standard** : It has become a widely adopted standard in the computer graphics industry, used in a vast array of applications, from video games and scientific visualization to virtual reality and augmented reality.
- **Open Source** : OpenGL's open-source nature has fostered a vibrant community of developers, contributing to its continuous evolution and improvement.

1.3 OpenGL's Role in Modern Graphics

OpenGL continues to play a vital role in modern computer graphics, serving as a foundation for many cutting-edge technologies and applications.

Key Roles:

- **Game Development:** OpenGL remains a cornerstone of game development, powering a wide range of titles, from indie games to AAA blockbusters. Its flexibility and performance make it an ideal choice for creating visually stunning and immersive gaming experiences.
- **Virtual Reality (VR) and Augmented Reality (AR):** OpenGL is essential for rendering realistic and interactive VR and AR environments. Its ability to handle complex 3D graphics and interact with sensors and input devices makes it well-suited for these emerging technologies.

- **Scientific Visualization:** OpenGL is used to visualize complex scientific data, such as medical images, weather patterns, and simulations of physical phenomena. Its ability to handle large datasets and render them in a visually meaningful way is crucial for scientific research and discovery.
- **Computer-Aided Design (CAD):** OpenGL is used in CAD software to create and manipulate 3D models of objects, from simple mechanical parts to complex architectural structures. Its precision and accuracy make it an invaluable tool for engineers and designers.
- **High-Performance Computing (HPC):** OpenGL is used in HPC applications to visualize and analyze massive datasets generated by simulations and experiments. Its ability to handle parallel processing and leverage the power of GPUs makes it well-suited for these demanding tasks.

Key Advantages:

- **Hardware Acceleration:** OpenGL leverages the power of GPUs to accelerate graphics rendering, enabling real-time performance for complex 3D graphics.
- **Cross-Platform Compatibility:** OpenGL's cross-platform nature allows developers to create graphics applications that can run on a wide range of devices and operating systems.
- **Flexibility and Extensibility:** OpenGL provides a flexible and extensible framework that can be adapted to meet the specific needs of different applications.
- **Large Community and Resources:** A large and active community of developers contributes to the ongoing development and improvement of OpenGL, providing a wealth of resources and support.

1.4 Setting Up Your Development Environment

To start developing with OpenGL, you'll need to set up a suitable development environment on your chosen operating system (Windows, macOS, or Linux). Here's a general guide:

1. Choose an IDE (Integrated Development Environment)

- **Popular Choices:**
    - **Visual Studio (Windows):** A powerful and feature-rich IDE with excellent support for C++ and OpenGL.
    - **CLion (Cross-Platform):** A robust C++ IDE from JetBrains, known for its intelligent code completion and debugging features.
    - **Code::Blocks (Cross-Platform):** A free and open-source IDE with good support for OpenGL.
    - **VS Code (Cross-Platform):** A lightweight and versatile code editor with excellent extensibility through extensions for C++ and OpenGL development.

2. Install a C++ Compiler

- **Windows:**
    - **MinGW:** A popular open-source compiler suite for Windows.
    - **Visual Studio:** Includes a built-in C++ compiler.
- **macOS:**
    - **clang:** The default compiler on macOS.
- **Linux:**
    - **GCC (GNU Compiler Collection):** A widely used and powerful compiler.

3. Obtain the OpenGL Libraries

- **System Libraries:** OpenGL libraries are often pre-installed on most modern operating systems.
- **Platform-Specific Libraries:** You might need to install platform-specific libraries or headers for OpenGL.

4. Install and Configure a Windowing System

- **GLFW:** A popular, cross-platform library for creating and managing windows, handling input, and managing OpenGL contexts.
- **SDL (Simple DirectMedia Layer):** Another versatile library for handling windowing, input, and multimedia.

5. Choose a Graphics Library (Optional)

- **GLAD:** A library that helps you load OpenGL functions dynamically, ensuring compatibility with different OpenGL versions.
- **GLEW (OpenGL Extension Wrangler):** Another library for managing OpenGL extensions.

General Steps:

1. **Install your chosen IDE and C++ compiler.**
2. **Install GLFW (or SDL) and any necessary OpenGL libraries.**
3. **Create a new C++ project in your IDE.**
4. **Include the necessary header files (e.g., glad.h, glfw3.h).**
5. **Start writing your OpenGL code!**

Example (Simplified GLFW initialization in C++):

C++

```cpp
#include <glad/glad.h>
```

```cpp
#include <GLFW/glfw3.h>

int main() {
    // ... (GLFW window creation and initialization) ...

    if (!gladLoadGLLoader((GLADloadproc)glfwGetProcAddress))
    {
        std::cerr << "Failed to initialize GLAD" << std::endl;
        return -1;
    }

    // ... (Your OpenGL rendering code) ...

    glfwTerminate();
    return 0;
}
```

1.5 Basic OpenGL Concepts: Vertices, Primitives, and Pipelines

OpenGL operates by processing geometric data and rendering it to the screen. Here are some core concepts:

1. Vertices

- **Definition:** Vertices are the fundamental building blocks of 3D objects. They represent points in 3D space, typically defined by their x, y, and z coordinates.
- **Attributes:** Vertices can have associated attributes, such as:
    - **Position:** The 3D coordinates of the vertex.
    - **Color:** The color of the vertex.
    - **Normal:** A vector that defines the surface orientation at the vertex, used for lighting calculations.
    - **Texture Coordinates:** Coordinates that map the vertex to a texture image.

2. Primitives

- **Definition:** Primitives are basic geometric shapes formed by connecting vertices.
- **Common Primitives:**
    - **Points:** Single vertices rendered as dots.
    - **Lines:** Sequences of vertices connected by straight lines.
    - **Triangles:** The most common primitive in OpenGL, forming the basis for polygons and complex shapes.
    - **Quads:** Four vertices forming a quadrilateral (though less common in modern OpenGL).

3. The OpenGL Pipeline

The OpenGL pipeline is a series of stages that process the geometric data and ultimately produce the final image on the screen.

- **Vertex Shader:**
    - The first stage in the pipeline.
    - Processes individual vertices, transforming their positions and calculating attributes.

- o Allows for custom vertex transformations, such as applying model, view, and projection matrices.
- **Primitive Assembly:**
  - o Assembles vertices into primitives (e.g., triangles).
  - o Performs primitive culling (e.g., backface culling) to improve performance.
- **Geometry Shader (Optional):**
  - o A programmable stage that can modify the geometry, such as generating new vertices or primitives.
- **Rasterization:**
  - o Converts primitives into fragments (pixels).
  - o Determines which pixels on the screen are covered by the primitive.
- **Fragment Shader:**
  - o Processes individual fragments, calculating their final color and depth.
  - o Allows for complex shading effects, such as lighting, texturing, and blending.
- **Depth Test:**
  - o Determines which fragments are visible based on their depth.
  - o Prevents overlapping fragments from incorrectly obscuring each other.
- **Blending:**
  - o Combines the color of the fragment with the color of the existing pixels in the framebuffer.
- **Framebuffer Operations:**
  - o Writes the final color and depth information to the framebuffer.

1.6 Your First OpenGL Program: A Simple Triangle

This section will guide you through creating a basic OpenGL program that renders a simple triangle to the screen.

1. Project Setup

- **Create a new C++ project** in your chosen IDE.
- **Include necessary headers:**

C++

```cpp
#include <glad/glad.h>
#include <GLFW/glfw3.h>
```

2. Vertex Shader

- **Create a vertex shader:**

OpenGL Shading Language

```glsl
#version 330 core
layout (location = 0) in vec3 aPos;

void main()
{
    gl_Position = vec4(aPos, 1.0);
}
```

- **Explanation:**

- #version 330 core: Specifies the version of GLSL (OpenGL Shading Language) used.
- layout (location = 0) in vec3 aPos;: Declares an input variable named aPos to receive vertex position data.
- gl_Position: A special output variable that defines the vertex position in clip space.

3. Fragment Shader

- **Create a fragment shader:**

OpenGL Shading Language

```glsl
#version 330 core
out vec4 FragColor;

void main()
{
    FragColor = vec4(1.0f, 0.5f, 0.2f, 1.0f);
}
```

- **Explanation:**
  - out vec4 FragColor;: Declares an output variable that specifies the color of the fragment.
  - FragColor = vec4(1.0f, 0.5f, 0.2f, 1.0f);: Sets the color of the fragment to orange (red, green, blue, alpha).

4. Vertex Data

- **Define vertex data:**

C++

```cpp
float vertices[] = {
    0.5f, -0.5f, 0.0f,
   -0.5f, -0.5f, 0.0f,
    0.0f,  0.5f, 0.0f
};
```

- **Create and bind a Vertex Buffer Object (VBO):**

C++

```cpp
unsigned int VBO;
glGenBuffers(1, &VBO);
glBindBuffer(GL_ARRAY_BUFFER, VBO);
glBufferData(GL_ARRAY_BUFFER, sizeof(vertices), vertices, GL_STATIC_DRAW);
```

5. Configure Vertex Attribute

- **Tell OpenGL how to interpret the vertex data:**

C++

```cpp
glVertexAttribPointer(0, 3, GL_FLOAT, GL_FALSE, 3 * sizeof(float), (void*)0);
glEnableVertexAttribArray(0);
```

6. Render Loop

- **Clear the screen and depth buffer:**

C++

```cpp
glClearColor(0.2f, 0.3f, 0.3f, 1.0f);
glClear(GL_COLOR_BUFFER_BIT | GL_DEPTH_BUFFER_BIT);
```

- **Draw the triangle:**

C++

```cpp
glDrawArrays(GL_TRIANGLES, 0, 3);
```

7. Swap Buffers

- **Swap front and back buffers:**

C++

```cpp
glfwSwapBuffers(window);
```

8. Event Handling

- **Handle window events (e.g., closing the window):**

C++

```cpp
while (!glfwWindowShouldClose(window))
{
    // ... (event handling and rendering loop) ...
```

}

This is a simplified example. You'll need to complete the GLFW window creation and initialization, compile and link your shaders, and handle error checking.

This basic example demonstrates the core steps involved in rendering graphics with OpenGL. You can build upon this foundation to create more complex scenes and applications.

2. OpenGL Fundamentals

2.1 Window Creation and Context Management

Before you can render any graphics with OpenGL, you need to create a window and an OpenGL context. The context is essentially the environment where OpenGL functions operate. It provides access to the GPU and its resources.

1. Choosing a Windowing Library

- **GLFW (Graphics Library Framework):** A popular, cross-platform library that simplifies window creation, input handling, and managing OpenGL contexts. It's known for its ease of use and portability.
- **SDL (Simple DirectMedia Layer):** Another versatile library that provides a broader range of functionalities beyond windowing, including audio, input, and image loading.

2. Creating a Window with GLFW

- **Initialize GLFW:**
- C++

```cpp
if (!glfwInit())
    return -1;
```

-
-

- **Set window hints:**
- C++

glfwWindowHint(GLFW_CONTEXT_VERSION_MAJOR, 3);

glfwWindowHint(GLFW_CONTEXT_VERSION_MINOR, 3);

glfwWindowHint(GLFW_OPENGL_PROFILE, GLFW_OPENGL_CORE_PROFILE);

-
  - These hints specify the desired OpenGL version and profile (core profile for modern OpenGL).
- **Create a window:**
- C++

GLFWwindow* window = glfwCreateWindow(800, 600, "My OpenGL Window", NULL, NULL);

if (window == NULL)

{

  glfwTerminate();

  return -1;

}

-
-

3. Creating an OpenGL Context

- **Make the window's context current:**
- C++

glfwMakeContextCurrent(window);

-
  - This makes the newly created OpenGL context active for subsequent OpenGL calls.
- **Initialize GLAD:**
- C++

```cpp
if (!gladLoadGLLoader((GLADloadproc)glfwGetProcAddress))
{
    std::cout << "Failed to initialize GLAD" << std::endl;
    return -1;
}
```

-
  - GLAD helps load OpenGL functions dynamically, ensuring compatibility with different OpenGL versions.

4. Event Handling

- **Process events:**
- C++

```cpp
while (!glfwWindowShouldClose(window))
{
    // Process input events (e.g., keyboard, mouse)
    glfwPollEvents();

    // ... (Your rendering code) ...

    glfwSwapBuffers(window);
```

}
-
  - glfwPollEvents() checks for and handles window events (e.g., closing, resizing).
  - glfwSwapBuffers() swaps the front and back buffers of the window, displaying the rendered image.

5. Terminating GLFW

- **Terminate GLFW:**
- C++

glfwTerminate();

-
-

Key Considerations:

- **Error Handling:** Always check for errors after each GLFW function call to ensure proper initialization and prevent unexpected behavior.
- **Context Management:** Ensure that only one context is current at a time.
- **Platform-Specific Considerations:** While GLFW aims for cross-platform compatibility, minor platform-specific adjustments might be necessary.

2.2 Shaders: Vertex and Fragment Shaders

Shaders are small programs that execute on the GPU during the rendering pipeline. They give developers fine-grained control over how vertices and fragments are processed, enabling a wide range of visual effects.

1. Vertex Shader

- **Purpose:**
    - Transforms the position of each vertex in 3D space.
    - Calculates and passes attributes (e.g., color, normal, texture coordinates) to the fragment shader.
- **Key Functions:**
    - **Position Transformation:** Applies transformations (model, view, projection matrices) to convert vertex positions from object space to clip space.
    - **Attribute Calculation:** Calculates and passes attributes (e.g., normals, tangents, texture coordinates) that are interpolated across the primitive for use in the fragment shader.
- **Example:**

OpenGL Shading Language

```glsl
#version 330 core
layout (location = 0) in vec3 aPos;

void main()
{
    gl_Position = vec4(aPos, 1.0);
}
```

2. Fragment Shader

- **Purpose:**
    - Determines the color of each fragment (pixel) that is covered by a primitive.
- **Key Functions:**
    - **Color Calculation:** Calculates the final color of the fragment based on various factors, such as:
        - Lighting calculations (ambient, diffuse, specular)
        - Texture sampling
        - Blending with other fragments
        - Special effects (e.g., fog, bloom)
- **Example:**

OpenGL Shading Language

```glsl
#version 330 core
out vec4 FragColor;

void main()
{
    FragColor = vec4(1.0f, 0.5f, 0.2f, 1.0f); // Set fragment color to orange
}
```

3. Shader Compilation and Linking

- **Create Shader Objects:**
    - Use glCreateShader() to create shader objects for the vertex and fragment shaders.
- **Attach Shader Source:**

- Use glShaderSource() to attach the shader source code to the corresponding shader objects.
- **Compile Shaders:**
  - Use glCompileShader() to compile the shader source code.
  - Check for compilation errors using glGetShaderiv() and glGetShaderInfoLog().
- **Create a Program Object:**
  - Use glCreateProgram() to create a program object.
- **Attach Shaders to Program:**
  - Use glAttachShader() to attach the compiled vertex and fragment shaders to the program object.
- **Link the Program:**
  - Use glLinkProgram() to link the shaders together.
  - Check for linking errors using glGetProgramiv() and glGetProgramInfoLog().
- **Use the Program:**
  - Use glUseProgram() to activate the linked program for rendering.

4. Shader Uniforms

- **Definition:** Uniforms are variables that can be set from the CPU and used within shaders.
- **Purpose:**
  - Control shader behavior dynamically (e.g., change material properties, adjust lighting parameters).
  - Pass data from the CPU to the GPU.
- **Example:**
  - In the vertex shader:
  - OpenGL Shading Language

uniform mat4 model;

```glsl
void main()
{
    gl_Position = model * vec4(aPos, 1.0);
}
```

-
-
  - In the C++ code:
  - C++

```cpp
glUniformMatrix4fv(glGetUniformLocation(shaderProgram, "model"), 1, GL_FALSE, glm::value_ptr(modelMatrix));
```

-
-

2.3 Data Buffers: Vertex Buffer Objects (VBOs)

VBOs are essential for efficiently storing and managing large amounts of vertex data in OpenGL.

1. Purpose

- **Efficient Data Transfer:** VBOs allow you to transfer vertex data (positions, colors, normals, etc.) from CPU memory to GPU memory in a single, efficient operation.
- **Data Caching:** The GPU can cache VBO data, significantly improving rendering performance, especially when drawing the same geometry multiple times.

2. Creating a VBO

- **Generate a VBO ID:**

- C++

unsigned int VBO;

glGenBuffers(1, &VBO);

-
-
- **Bind the VBO:**
- C++

glBindBuffer(GL_ARRAY_BUFFER, VBO);

-
  - This makes the specified VBO the active buffer for subsequent buffer operations.
- **Transfer Data to VBO:**
- C++

```
float vertices[] = {
  // ... your vertex data ...
};
```

glBufferData(GL_ARRAY_BUFFER, sizeof(vertices), vertices, GL_STATIC_DRAW);

-
  - glBufferData() transfers the vertex data from CPU memory to the GPU's memory.
    - GL_STATIC_DRAW: Indicates that the data will be used frequently and won't change often.
    - Other usage hints include GL_DYNAMIC_DRAW (data may change

frequently) and GL_STREAM_DRAW (data will be used once and then discarded).

3. Using Vertex Data with VBOs

- **Specify Vertex Attribute Pointers:**
- C++

glVertexAttribPointer(0, 3, GL_FLOAT, GL_FALSE, 3 * sizeof(float), (void*)0);

glEnableVertexAttribArray(0);

-
    - glVertexAttribPointer() tells OpenGL how to interpret the vertex data stored in the VBO.
        - 0: Specifies the index of the vertex attribute (matches layout (location = 0) in the vertex shader).
        - 3: Specifies the number of components per vertex attribute (x, y, z).
        - GL_FLOAT: Specifies the data type of each component.
        - GL_FALSE: Specifies whether the data should be normalized (not normalized in this case).
        - 3 * sizeof(float): Specifies the stride (byte offset) between consecutive vertex attributes.
        - (void*)0: Specifies the offset of the first component of the vertex attribute within the buffer.

4. Unbinding the VBO

- **Unbind the VBO to avoid unintended modifications:**
- C++

glBindBuffer(GL_ARRAY_BUFFER, 0);

-
-

5. Deleting the VBO

- **Delete the VBO when it's no longer needed:**
- C++

glDeleteBuffers(1, &VBO);

-
-

2.4 Index Buffers: Element Buffer Objects (EBOs)

EBOs are used to efficiently render the same vertex data multiple times, especially when dealing with complex meshes that share vertices.

1. Purpose

- **Reduced Data Redundancy:** Instead of storing duplicate vertex data for shared vertices, EBOs store indices that refer to vertices in a separate vertex buffer.
- **Improved Rendering Performance:** By reducing the amount of data that needs to be transferred to the GPU and processed, EBOs can significantly improve rendering performance, especially for large meshes.

2. Creating an EBO

- **Generate an EBO ID:**
- C++

```cpp
unsigned int EBO;
glGenBuffers(1, &EBO);
```

-
-
- **Bind the EBO:**
- C++

```cpp
glBindBuffer(GL_ELEMENT_ARRAY_BUFFER, EBO);
```

-
-
- **Transfer Index Data to EBO:**
- C++

```cpp
unsigned int indices[] = {
    // ... indices of vertices to be drawn (e.g., 0, 1, 2 for a triangle) ...
};
glBufferData(GL_ELEMENT_ARRAY_BUFFER, sizeof(indices), indices, GL_STATIC_DRAW);
```

-
-

3. Rendering with an EBO

- **Use glDrawElements() to render:**
- C++

```cpp
glDrawElements(GL_TRIANGLES, 6, GL_UNSIGNED_INT, 0);
```

-
  - GL_TRIANGLES: Specifies the primitive type.
  - 6: Specifies the number of indices to be drawn.

- o GL_UNSIGNED_INT: Specifies the data type of the indices.
- o 0: Specifies the offset of the first index in the EBO.

4. Unbinding the EBO

- **Unbind the EBO to avoid unintended modifications:**
- C++

glBindBuffer(GL_ELEMENT_ARRAY_BUFFER, 0);

-
-

5. Deleting the EBO

- **Delete the EBO when it's no longer needed:**
- C++

glDeleteBuffers(1, &EBO);

-
-

Example

For a simple triangle, you might have the following:

- **Vertices:**
- C++

```
float vertices[] = {
    0.5f,  0.5f, 0.0f,  // top right
    0.5f, -0.5f, 0.0f,  // bottom right
   -0.5f, -0.5f, 0.0f,  // bottom left
```

    -0.5f, 0.5f, 0.0f // top left
};

-
-
- **Indices:**[1]
- C++

```
unsigned int indices[] = {
    0, 1, 3,  // First Triangle
    1, 2, 3   // Second Triangle
};
```

-

2.5 Transformations: Translation, Rotation, Scaling

Transformations are operations that change the position, size, or orientation of objects in 3D space. They are crucial for manipulating and positioning objects within your scene.

1. Translation

- **Definition:** Shifts an object's position along the x, y, and z axes.
- **Matrix Representation:**

[1 0 0 tx]
[0 1 0 ty]
[0 0 1 tz]

[0 0 0 1]

-
  - tx, ty, and tz represent the translation amounts along the x, y, and z axes, respectively.

2. Rotation

- **Definition:** Rotates an object around a specific axis.
- **Matrix Representations:**
  - **Rotation around X-axis:**

[1 0   0   ]
[0 cos(angle) -sin(angle)]
[0 sin(angle) cos(angle)]

  -
  -
  - **Rotation around Y-axis:**

[cos(angle) 0 sin(angle)]
[0   1 0   ]
[-sin(angle) 0 cos(angle)]

  -
  -
  - **Rotation around Z-axis:**

[cos(angle) -sin(angle) 0]
[sin(angle) cos(angle) 0]
[0   0   1]

  -

-
  - angle is the rotation angle in radians.

3. Scaling

- **Definition:** Changes the size of an object along the x, y, and z axes.
- **Matrix Representation:**

$$\begin{bmatrix} sx & 0 & 0 \\ 0 & sy & 0 \\ 0 & 0 & sz \end{bmatrix}$$

-
  - sx, sy, and sz represent the scaling factors along the x, y, and z axes, respectively.

4. Combining Transformations

- Transformations can be combined by multiplying their corresponding matrices.
- The order of matrix multiplication matters! The order of transformations affects the final result.

5. Applying Transformations in OpenGL

- **Model Matrix:** Represents transformations applied to the object itself (e.g., scaling, rotation, translation).
- **View Matrix:** Represents the camera's position and orientation in the world.
- **Projection Matrix:** Represents the transformation from 3D world coordinates to 2D screen coordinates.
- **In the Vertex Shader:**
- OpenGL Shading Language

```glsl
uniform mat4 model;
uniform mat4 view;
uniform mat4 projection;

void main()
{
    gl_Position = projection * view * model * vec4(aPos, 1.0);
}
```

-
-
- **In[1] C++ Code:**
- C++

```cpp
glm::mat4 model = glm::mat4(1.0f);
model = glm::rotate(model, glm::radians(angle), glm::vec3(0.0f, 1.0f, 0.0f));
// ... other transformations ...

glUniformMatrix4fv(glGetUniformLocation(shaderProgram, "model"), 1, GL_FALSE, glm::value_ptr(model));
```

-
-

2.6 Matrices: Model, View, and Projection Matrices

Matrices are fundamental for performing transformations in 3D graphics. They provide a concise and efficient way to represent and combine various transformations.

1. Model Matrix

- **Purpose:** Represents transformations applied to the object itself within its own local coordinate system.
- **Transformations:**
    - **Translation:** Shifts the object's position.
    - **Rotation:** Rotates the object around a specific axis.
    - **Scaling:** Changes the object's size.
    - **Other transformations:** Skewing, shearing, etc.
- **Example:**
- C++

glm::mat4 model = glm::mat4(1.0f);

model = glm::translate(model, glm::vec3(1.0f, 0.5f, 0.0f));

model = glm::rotate(model, glm::radians(45.0f), glm::vec3(0.0f, 1.0f, 0.0f));

-
-

2. View Matrix

- **Purpose:** Represents the camera's position and orientation in the world.
- **Transformations:**
    - **Translation:** Positions the camera at a specific point in the world.
    - **Rotation:** Orients the camera to look at a specific point (target).

- **Often calculated using the "LookAt" function:**
  - C++

```cpp
glm::mat4 view = glm::lookAt(cameraPos, cameraTarget, cameraUp);
```

  -
  -

3. Projection Matrix

- **Purpose:** Transforms 3D world coordinates into 2D screen coordinates.
- **Types of Projections:**
  - **Perspective Projection:** Creates a sense of depth and perspective, making objects appear smaller as they move further away.
  - **Orthographic Projection:** Projects objects onto a plane without any perspective distortion.
- **Example (Perspective Projection):**
- C++

```cpp
glm::mat4 projection = glm::perspective(glm::radians(45.0f), screenWidth / screenHeight, 0.1f, 100.0f);
```

-
  - fov: Field of view in degrees.
  - aspectRatio: Aspect ratio of the viewport (width / height).
  - nearPlane: Distance to the near clipping plane.
  - farPlane: Distance to the far clipping plane.

4. Combining Matrices in the Vertex Shader

- **Order of Transformations:**

1. **Model -> View -> Projection**
   - OpenGL Shading Language

```
uniform mat4 model;
uniform mat4 view;
uniform mat4 projection;

void main()
{
    gl_Position = projection * view * model * vec4(aPos, 1.0);
}
```

-
-
- **Explanation:**[1]
    1. **Model:** Transforms the vertex from object space to world space.
    2. **View:** Transforms the vertex from world space to camera space (eye space).
    3. **Projection:** Transforms the vertex from camera space to clip space, and finally to normalized device coordinates (NDC).

3. Lighting and Materials

3.1 Light Sources: Ambient, Diffuse, Specular

Lighting is crucial for creating realistic and visually appealing 3D scenes. It simulates how light interacts with objects in the real world, influencing their appearance and creating depth and dimension.

1. Light Sources

- **Ambient Light:**
    - Represents the general, non-directional illumination in the scene.
    - Simulates the overall brightness of the environment, such as light bouncing off walls and ceilings.
    - Typically a constant color that affects all objects equally.
- **Diffuse Light:**
    - Represents light that is scattered evenly in all directions when it hits a surface.
    - Creates a uniform brightness across the surface of the object.
    - The intensity of diffuse lighting depends on the angle between the surface normal and the light direction.
- **Specular Light:**
    - Represents the bright highlight that appears on a surface when light reflects directly towards the viewer.
    - Creates a sense of shininess and realism.

- The intensity and position of specular highlights depend on the viewer's position, the light direction, and the surface's material properties (e.g., shininess).

2. Light Properties

- **Position:** The location of the light source in world space.
- **Direction:** The direction in which the light is shining (for directional lights).
- **Color:** The color of the light source.
- **Intensity:** The brightness of the light source.

3. Implementing Lighting in OpenGL

- **In the Fragment Shader:**
    - Calculate the diffuse and specular lighting components for each fragment.
    - Combine the ambient, diffuse, and specular components to determine the final color of the fragment.

Example (Simplified Diffuse Lighting Calculation):

OpenGL Shading Language

```glsl
vec3 norm = normalize(Normal);
vec3 lightDir = normalize(lightPos - FragPos);
float diff = max(dot(norm, lightDir), 0.0);
vec3 diffuse = diff * lightColor;
```

Key Considerations:

- **Light Attenuation:** Simulates the decrease in light intensity as the distance from the light source increases.

- **Multiple Lights:** You can incorporate multiple light sources (ambient, directional, point, spot) to create more complex and realistic lighting scenarios.

3.2 Materials: Properties and Lighting Models

Materials define the visual appearance of objects in a 3D scene. They determine how light interacts with the object's surface, influencing its color, shininess, and overall appearance.

1. Material Properties

- **Ambient Reflectivity:** Determines how much ambient light the material reflects.
- **Diffuse Reflectivity:** Determines how much diffuse light the material reflects.
- **Specular Reflectivity:** Determines how much specular light the material reflects.
- **Shininess:** Controls the sharpness and intensity of specular highlights. Higher shininess values result in sharper, more intense highlights.

2. Lighting Models

Lighting models describe the mathematical calculations used to determine how light interacts with a surface.

- **Phong Lighting Model:**
    - A classic and widely used lighting model.
    - Calculates diffuse and specular lighting based on the angle between the surface normal, light direction, and view direction.
- **Blinn-Phong Lighting Model:**
    - An improvement over the Phong model.

- Calculates specular lighting more efficiently by using a halfway vector between the light direction and the view direction.

3. Implementing Materials in OpenGL

- **In the Vertex Shader:**
    - Pass material properties (e.g., ambient, diffuse, specular, shininess) to the fragment shader.
- **In the Fragment Shader:**
    - Use the material properties and lighting calculations to determine the final color of the fragment.

Example (Simplified Phong Lighting Calculation):

OpenGL Shading Language

```glsl
vec3 ambient = ambientStrength * lightColor;
vec3 norm = normalize(Normal);
vec3 lightDir = normalize(lightPos - FragPos);
float diff = max(dot(norm, lightDir), 0.0);
vec3 diffuse = diff * lightColor;
vec3 viewDir = normalize(cameraPos - FragPos);
vec3 halfwayDir = normalize(lightDir + viewDir);
float spec = pow(max(dot(norm, halfwayDir), 0.0), shininess);
vec3 specular = specularStrength * lightColor * spec;
vec3 result = ambient + diffuse + specular;
FragColor = vec4(result, 1.0);
```

Key Considerations:

- **Material Textures:** Textures can be used to add detail and realism to materials by varying their properties (e.g., color, roughness, normal) across the surface of the object.
- **Advanced Techniques:** More advanced techniques like physically-based rendering (PBR) provide more accurate and realistic lighting and material models.

By understanding material properties and implementing appropriate lighting models, you can create visually stunning and realistic 3D scenes that accurately simulate the interaction of light with objects.

3.3 Phong Shading and Blinn-Phong Shading

These are classic lighting models used to calculate the appearance of surfaces in 3D graphics.

1. Phong Shading

- **Core Concept:**
    - Calculates diffuse and specular reflections based on the angle between the surface normal, light direction, and view direction.
- **Diffuse Reflection:**
    - Proportional to the cosine of the angle between the surface normal and the light direction.
    - Simulates how light scatters evenly across the surface.
- **Specular Reflection:**
    - Proportional to the cosine of the angle between the reflection vector and the view direction, raised to a power (shininess exponent).
    - Simulates the bright highlight that appears on a shiny surface.

- **Limitations:**
    - Can be computationally expensive, especially for high shininess values.
    - Can sometimes produce artifacts, such as "fireflies" (bright spots) in the specular highlights.

2. Blinn-Phong Shading

- **Core Concept:**
    - An optimization of the Phong model.
    - Introduces the "halfway vector," which is the vector halfway between the light direction and the view direction.
- **Specular Reflection:**
    - Proportional to the cosine of the angle between the surface normal and the halfway vector, raised to a power (shininess exponent).
- **Advantages:**
    - More efficient than Phong shading, especially for high shininess values.
    - Produces smoother and more realistic specular highlights.

3. Implementation

- **In the Fragment Shader:**
- OpenGL Shading Language

```
// Phong Shading

float spec = pow(max(dot(reflect(-lightDir, norm), viewDir), 0.0), shininess);


// Blinn-Phong Shading
```

```
vec3 halfwayDir = normalize(lightDir + viewDir);
float spec = pow(max(dot(norm, halfwayDir), 0.0), shininess);
```

-
-

4. Key Considerations:

- **Shininess Exponent:** Controls the sharpness and intensity of the specular highlights. Higher values result in sharper highlights.
- **Material Properties:** The material properties (ambient, diffuse, specular, shininess) significantly influence the final appearance of the object.

Both Phong and Blinn-Phong shading models are widely used in 3D graphics, providing a solid foundation for creating realistic and visually appealing lighting effects. Blinn-Phong shading is generally preferred due to its efficiency and improved results.

3.4 Lighting Techniques: Directional, Point, and Spot Lights

1. Directional Lights

- **Characteristics:**
    - Simulate light sources that are infinitely far away, such as the sun.
    - Have a constant direction but no specific position.
    - Often used to simulate ambient or sunlight in a scene.
- **Implementation:**
    - Define a constant light direction vector in the shader.

2. Point Lights

- **Characteristics:**
  - Simulate light sources that emit light in all directions from a specific point, such as a light bulb.
  - Have a position in world space.
  - Light intensity decreases with distance from the light source.
- **Implementation:**
  - Calculate the vector from the fragment's position to the light source's position.
  - Apply attenuation to the light intensity based on the distance.

3. Spot Lights

- **Characteristics:**
  - Simulate lights that emit light within a cone, such as a flashlight.
  - Have a position, direction, and an inner and outer cone angle.
  - Light intensity decreases with distance from the light source and outside the cone.
- **Implementation:**
  - Calculate the vector from the fragment's position to the light source's position.
  - Calculate the angle between the light direction and the vector to the fragment.
  - Apply attenuation based on the distance and the angle.

4. Combining Light Sources

- You can combine multiple light sources (directional, point, spot) to create more complex and realistic lighting scenarios.
- The final color of a fragment is typically calculated by summing the contributions from all light sources.

Example (Point Light Calculation):

OpenGL Shading Language

```glsl
vec3 lightDir = normalize(lightPos - FragPos);
float distance = length(lightPos - FragPos);
float attenuation = 1.0 / (1.0 + distance * distance); // Simple distance attenuation

vec3 diffuse = diff * lightColor * attenuation;
// ... (specular calculation) ...
```

Part 2: Advanced Techniques

4. Textures and Sampling

4.1 Texture Mapping: 2D, 3D, and Cube Maps

Textures are images that are applied to the surfaces of 3D objects, adding visual detail and realism.[1]

1. 2D Textures

- **Most Common Type:** The most widely used type of texture, representing a flat, 2D image.
- **Application:** Applied to the surfaces of 3D objects to add color, patterns, and details.[2]
- **Texture Coordinates:** Each vertex of a 3D model is assigned a set of texture coordinates (typically (u, v)), which specify the location within the texture image that should be mapped to that vertex.[3]

2. 3D Textures

- **Representation:** Store color or other data within a 3D volume.[4]
- **Applications:**
    - Used for effects like volumetric fog, clouds, and smoke.
    - Can also be used for storing data such as density fields or temperature distributions.

3. Cube Maps

- **Representation:** A collection of six 2D textures, each representing one face of a cube.[5]
- **Applications:**
  - Used to simulate reflections and environments.[6]
  - The six faces of the cube map represent the colors of the environment in different directions.
  - Commonly used for skyboxes to create immersive environments.[7]

4. Texture Sampling

- **Process:** The process of retrieving color or other data from a texture based on texture coordinates.[8]
- **Interpolation:** Textures are typically stored at a finite resolution. Interpolation techniques (e.g., bilinear, trilinear) are used to determine the color of fragments that fall between texture pixels.
- **Filtering:** Techniques used to smooth out aliasing artifacts that can occur when sampling textures at different levels of detail.
  - **Mipmapping:** Creates a hierarchy of lower-resolution versions of the texture, allowing the GPU to select the appropriate level of detail based on the distance to the object.[9]
  - **Anisotropic Filtering:** Improves image quality when viewing textures at oblique angles.[10]

5. Implementing Textures in OpenGL

- **Create a Texture Object:**
- C++

```
unsigned int texture;
glGenTextures(1, &texture);
```

glBindTexture(GL_TEXTURE_2D, texture);

-
-
- **Load and Set Texture Data:**
- C++

// Load image data (e.g., using stb_image.h library)

glTexImage2D(GL_TEXTURE_2D, 0, GL_RGB, width, height, 0, GL_RGB, GL_UNSIGNED_BYTE, data);

-
-
- **Generate Mipmaps:**
- C++

glGenerateMipmap(GL_TEXTURE_2D);

-
-
- **Set Texture Parameters:**
- C++

glTexParameteri(GL_TEXTURE_2D, GL_TEXTURE_WRAP_S, GL_REPEAT);

glTexParameteri(GL_TEXTURE_2D, GL_TEXTURE_WRAP_T, GL_REPEAT);

glTexParameteri(GL_TEXTURE_2D, GL_TEXTURE_MIN_FILTER, GL_LINEAR_MIPMAP_LINEAR);

glTexParameteri(GL_TEXTURE_2D, GL_TEXTURE_MAG_FILTER, GL_LINEAR);

-
-
- **Use Textures in the Fragment Shader:**
- OpenGL Shading Language

out vec4 FragColor;

in vec2 TexCoords;

uniform sampler2D ourTexture;

void main()
{
   FragColor = texture(ourTexture, TexCoords);
}

-
-

4.2 Texture Filtering: Mipmapping and Anisotropic Filtering

1. Mipmapping

- **Purpose:** To reduce aliasing artifacts (jagged edges) that occur when sampling textures from a distance.
- **Concept:**
    - Creates a "mipmap chain" - a hierarchy of pre-generated, lower-resolution versions of the original texture.

- When sampling a texture, the GPU selects the mipmap level that best matches the size of the texture on the screen.
- **Benefits:**
  - Significantly reduces aliasing artifacts, such as shimmering and flickering.
  - Improves rendering performance by reducing the number of texture samples required.

2. Anisotropic Filtering

- **Purpose:** To improve image quality when viewing textures at oblique angles.
- **Concept:**
  - Samples multiple mipmap levels along the direction of anisotropy (the direction in which the texture is stretched or skewed).
  - Combines the samples to create a more accurate and detailed image.
- **Benefits:**
  - Eliminates blurring and distortion that occurs when viewing textures at sharp angles.
  - Provides higher image quality, especially for highly detailed textures.

3. Implementation

- **Enable Mipmapping:**
- C++

glGenerateMipmap(GL_TEXTURE_2D);

-
-
- **Set Texture Filtering Parameters:**

- C++

glTexParameteri(GL_TEXTURE_2D, GL_TEXTURE_MIN_FILTER, GL_LINEAR_MIPMAP_LINEAR);

glTexParameteri(GL_TEXTURE_2D, GL_TEXTURE_MAG_FILTER, GL_LINEAR);

-
  - GL_LINEAR_MIPMAP_LINEAR: Performs linear interpolation between mipmap levels.
- **Enable Anisotropic Filtering (if supported):**
- C++

GLfloat maxAnisotropy;

glGetFloatv(GL_MAX_TEXTURE_MAX_ANISOTROPY_EXT, &maxAnisotropy);

glTexParameterf(GL_TEXTURE_2D, GL_TEXTURE_MAX_ANISOTROPY_EXT, maxAnisotropy);

-
-

4. Considerations:

- **Performance:** Anisotropic filtering can be computationally expensive, especially at high levels.
- **GPU Support:** The level of anisotropic filtering support varies between GPUs.

4.3 Texture Coordinates and Sampling

1. Texture Coordinates

- **Definition:**
  - A set of coordinates (typically (u, v)) that specify the location within a texture image that should be mapped to a particular point on the surface of a 3D object.
  - Usually defined in the range of 0.0 to 1.0, where (0.0, 0.0) represents the bottom-left corner of the texture and (1.0, 1.0) represents the top-right corner.
- **Assignment:**
  - Texture coordinates are typically assigned to vertices of a 3D model.
  - These coordinates are then interpolated across the surface of the object during rendering.
- **Example:**
- C++

```
float vertices[] = {
    // positions      // colors         // texture coords
    0.5f,  0.5f, 0.0f, 1.0f, 0.0f, 0.0f, 1.0f, 1.0f,  // top right
    0.5f, -0.5f, 0.0f, 0.0f, 1.0f, 0.0f, 1.0f, 0.0f,  // bottom right
   -0.5f, -0.5f, 0.0f, 0.0f, 0.0f, 1.0f, 0.0f, 0.0f,  // bottom left
   -0.5f,  0.5f, 0.0f, 1.0f, 1.0f, 1.0f, 0.0f, 1.0f   // top left
};
```

-
-

2. Texture Sampling

- **Process:**

- o In the fragment shader, the texture coordinates of the current fragment are used to look up the corresponding color from the texture image.
- o This involves determining the location within the texture image that corresponds to the fragment's coordinates.
- **Interpolation:**
  - o If the fragment falls between texture pixels, interpolation is used to determine the final color.
    - ■ **Bilinear Interpolation:** Interpolates between the colors of the four nearest texture pixels.
    - ■ **Trilinear Interpolation:** Interpolates between the colors of the four nearest texture pixels across multiple mipmap levels.
- **Example (in Fragment Shader):**
- OpenGL Shading Language

```glsl
out vec4 FragColor;
in vec2 TexCoords;

uniform sampler2D ourTexture;

void main()
{
    FragColor = texture(ourTexture, TexCoords);
}
```

-
-

3. Advanced Techniques

- **Texture Wrapping:**
  - Determines how the texture is sampled when the texture coordinates fall outside the range [0, 1].
    - GL_REPEAT: Repeats the texture seamlessly.
    - GL_MIRRORED_REPEAT: Repeats the texture with mirroring.
    - GL_CLAMP_TO_EDGE: Clamps the texture coordinates to the edge of the texture.
- **Texture Blending:**
  - Combines multiple textures using blending functions.
  - Used to create effects like transparency, masking, and layering.

4.4 Texture Blending and Operations

1. Texture Blending

- **Purpose:** To combine multiple textures to create more complex and interesting visual effects.
- **Techniques:**
  - **Alpha Blending:**
    - Combines the color of a fragment with the color of the existing pixels in the framebuffer based on an alpha value.
    - Used to create transparent or semi-transparent objects.
  - **Multiply Blending:**
    - Multiplies the color of the fragment with the color of the existing pixels in the framebuffer.
    - Can be used to darken or lighten the existing color.
  - **Add Blending:**

- Adds the color of the fragment to the color of the existing pixels in the framebuffer.
- Can be used to create glowing or additive effects.
- **Implementation:**
    - Use glBlendFunc() to specify the blending function.
    - For example, glBlendFunc(GL_SRC_ALPHA, GL_ONE_MINUS_SRC_ALPHA) for alpha blending.

2. Texture Operations

- **Purpose:** To perform operations on texture data before or after sampling.
- **Techniques:**
    - **Texture Swizzling:** Rearranges or modifies the components of a texture (e.g., swapping red and blue channels).
    - **Texture Lookups:** Perform additional texture lookups based on the current texture coordinates.
    - **Color Space Conversions:** Convert texture data between different color spaces (e.g., RGB to HSV).
- **Implementation:**
    - Can be implemented using shader code or through hardware-specific texture units.

3. Examples

- **Transparency:** Render objects with transparent textures using alpha blending.
- **Decals:** Apply decals (e.g., stickers, graffiti) to surfaces using alpha blending and texture masking.

- **Bump Mapping:** Simulate surface bumps and irregularities by modulating the surface normal based on a heightmap texture.
- **Normal Mapping:** Store surface normal information in a texture to enhance lighting and shading effects.

4. **Considerations**

- **Performance:** Texture blending and operations can increase the computational cost of rendering.
- **Hardware Support:** The specific blending functions and texture operations supported can vary between GPUs.

5. Geometry Shaders and Tessellation

5.1 Geometry Shader Concepts and Applications

Geometry Shaders are a programmable stage in the OpenGL pipeline that provide a high degree of flexibility and control over the rendering process.

1. Concepts

- **Purpose:**
  - Operate on entire geometric primitives (points, lines, triangles) as input.
  - Can generate new vertices, primitives, or discard existing primitives.
  - Provide a powerful tool for manipulating and modifying geometry on the GPU.
- **Input:**
  - Receives a set of vertices that define a primitive (e.g., all vertices of a triangle).
  - Access to primitive-level information (e.g., adjacency information for neighboring primitives).
- **Output:**
  - Can emit new vertices and create new primitives (points, lines, triangles).
  - Can discard the input primitive entirely.
- **Flexibility:**
  - Allows for a wide range of geometric operations:

- **Primitive Refinement:** Subdividing primitives into smaller ones for more detailed rendering.
- **Instancing:** Creating multiple instances of a single object.
- **Level of Detail (LOD) Control:** Adjusting the level of detail of objects based on their distance from the viewer.
- **Procedural Geometry Generation:** Creating complex shapes and structures on the fly.

2. Applications

- **Tessellation:**
  - Subdividing surfaces into smaller triangles for smoother rendering.
  - Used to create highly detailed models with smooth curves and surfaces.
- **Instancing:**
  - Efficiently rendering multiple instances of the same object by processing the geometry once and then applying transformations to each instance.
- **Particle Systems:**
  - Generating and manipulating particles for effects like smoke, fire, and explosions.
- **Level of Detail (LOD) Control:**
  - Adaptively adjusting the complexity of objects based on their distance from the viewer, improving performance.
- **Procedural Geometry:**
  - Generating complex shapes and structures, such as trees, terrain, and clouds, on the fly.

3. Implementation

- **Create a Geometry Shader Object:**
  - Similar to creating vertex and fragment shaders.
- **Specify Input and Output Primitives:**
  - Define the input and output primitive types (e.g., layout (triangles) in; layout (triangle_strip) out;).
- **Access Input Data:**
  - Access input vertices and primitive-level information within the geometry shader.
- **Emit Vertices:**
  - Use the EmitVertex() function to emit new vertices.
  - Use the EndPrimitive() function to signal the end of a primitive.

4. Considerations

- **Performance:** Geometry shaders can be computationally expensive, especially when processing large amounts of geometry.
- **Hardware Support:** The level of geometry shader support can vary between GPUs.

Geometry Shaders provide a powerful tool for manipulating and modifying geometry on the GPU, enabling a wide range of creative and performance-enhancing techniques.

5.2 Tessellation Control and Evaluation Shaders

Tessellation is a powerful technique within OpenGL that allows for the dynamic subdivision of surfaces into smaller polygons, resulting in smoother and more detailed rendering. It involves two specialized shader stages:

1. Tessellation Control Shader (TCS)

- **Purpose:**
    - Controls the level of tessellation for each patch of geometry.
    - Receives a set of control points that define a patch (e.g., a quad).
    - Determines the tessellation factors for each edge of the patch.
    - Tessellation factors specify how many times each edge should be subdivided.
- **Inputs:**
    - Control points of the input patch.
    - Primitive-level information (e.g., patch ID).
- **Outputs:**
    - Tessellation factors for each edge of the patch.
    - Optional per-vertex data that is passed to the tessellation evaluation shader.
- **Example:**
- OpenGL Shading Language

```glsl
layout (vertices = 3) out; // For a triangle patch

void main()
{
  if (gl_InvocationID == 0) {
    // Calculate tessellation factors based on distance, etc.
    gl_TessLevelOuter[0] = 20.0;
    gl_TessLevelOuter[1] = 20.0;
    gl_TessLevelOuter[2] = 20.0;
    gl_TessLevelInner[0] = 20.0;
```

                }
        }

-
-

2. Tessellation Evaluation Shader (TES)

- **Purpose:**
    - Generates new vertices within the tessellated patch.
    - Interpolate vertex attributes (e.g., position, normal, texture coordinates) across the patch.
- **Inputs:**
    - Barycentric coordinates (u, v) within the tessellated patch.
    - Tessellation factors from the tessellation control shader.
    - Optional per-vertex data from the tessellation control shader.
- **Outputs:**
    - Positions and attributes of the generated vertices.
- **Example:**
- OpenGL Shading Language

```
layout (isolines, equal_spacing, ccw) in;

void main()
{
    // Interpolate position based on barycentric coordinates
    gl_Position = mix(mix(gl_in[0].gl_Position, gl_in[1].gl_Position, gl_TessCoord.x),
```

```
                    mix(gl_in[1].gl_Position, gl_in[2].gl_Position,
gl_TessCoord.x),
              gl_TessCoord.y);
}
```

-
-

3. Applications

- **Smooth Surfaces:** Creating smooth, curved surfaces from coarse polygonal meshes.
- **Level of Detail:** Adaptively tessellating surfaces based on distance or other factors.
- **Terrain Generation:** Generating detailed terrain landscapes.
- **Procedural Modeling:** Creating complex shapes and structures using tessellation techniques.

4. Considerations

- **Performance:** Tessellation can be computationally expensive, especially for highly tessellated surfaces.
- **Hardware Support:** The level of tessellation support can vary between GPUs.

5.3 Creating Tessellated Surfaces: Patches and Levels of Detail

Tessellation in OpenGL involves subdividing surfaces into smaller polygons, typically triangles. This is achieved by defining patches of geometry and controlling the level of tessellation for each patch.

1. Patches

- **Definition:** A patch is a collection of control points that define a surface.
- **Common Patch Types:**
  - **Triangles:** Defined by three control points.
  - **Quads:** Defined by four control points.
  - **Bezier Patches:** Defined by a set of control points that influence the shape of the surface.
- **Tessellation:**
  - The process of subdividing a patch into smaller triangles or quadrilaterals.
  - The number of subdivisions determines the level of detail of the tessellated surface.

2. Levels of Detail (LOD)

- **Dynamic Tessellation:** The level of tessellation can be adjusted dynamically based on various factors, such as:
  - **Distance from the Camera:** Higher levels of detail are used for objects closer to the camera, and lower levels of detail are used for objects farther away.
  - **View Direction:** Higher levels of detail are used for surfaces that are facing the camera directly.
  - **Screen Space Error:** Tessellate surfaces until the error between the tessellated surface and the original surface falls below a certain threshold.
- **Implementation:**
  - In the Tessellation Control Shader:
    - Calculate tessellation factors based on distance, view direction, or other criteria.
    - Adjust tessellation factors dynamically to achieve the desired level of detail.

3. Example (Distance-Based Tessellation)

OpenGL Shading Language

```glsl
// In Tessellation Control Shader
layout (vertices = 3) out;

void main()
{
    float distance = length(gl_in[0].gl_Position.xyz - cameraPosition);
    float tessLevel = 100.0f / distance; // Higher tessellation for closer objects

    gl_TessLevelOuter[0] = tessLevel;
    gl_TessLevelOuter[1] = tessLevel;
    gl_TessLevelOuter[2] = tessLevel;
    gl_TessLevelInner[0] = tessLevel;
}
```

4. Considerations

- **Performance:** Dynamic tessellation can be computationally expensive, especially for complex scenes with many tessellated surfaces.
- **Visual Quality:** The choice of tessellation factors and the implementation of LOD strategies significantly impact the visual quality and performance of the rendered scene.

6. Framebuffers and Render Targets

6.1 Framebuffer Objects (FBOs): Creating and Using

Framebuffers in OpenGL provide a mechanism for rendering to destinations other than the default framebuffer associated with the window. This powerful technique opens up a wide range of possibilities, including:

- **Render-to-Texture (RTT):** Rendering the scene to a texture instead of directly to the screen.
- **Post-processing Effects:** Applying effects like bloom, depth of field, and motion blur after the initial rendering pass.
- **Multiple Render Passes:** Performing rendering in multiple stages, using the output of one pass as input for the next.

1. Creating a Framebuffer Object

- **Generate an FBO:**
- C++

```cpp
unsigned int fbo;
glGenFramebuffers(1, &fbo);
glBindFramebuffer(GL_FRAMEBUFFER, fbo);
```

-
-

2. Creating Color Attachments

- **Create a Texture for Color Attachment:**
- C++

```cpp
unsigned int textureColorBuffer;
glGenTextures(1, &textureColorBuffer);
glBindTexture(GL_TEXTURE_2D, textureColorBuffer);
// Set texture parameters (e.g., size, format)
glTexImage2D(GL_TEXTURE_2D, 0, GL_RGB, width, height, 0, GL_RGB, GL_UNSIGNED_BYTE, NULL);
glTexParameteri(GL_TEXTURE_2D, GL_TEXTURE_MIN_FILTER, GL_LINEAR);
glTexParameteri(GL_TEXTURE_2D, GL_TEXTURE_MAG_FILTER, GL_LINEAR);
```

-
-
- **Attach Texture[1] to FBO:**
- C++

```cpp
glFramebufferTexture2D(GL_FRAMEBUFFER, GL_COLOR_ATTACHMENT0, GL_TEXTURE_2D, textureColorBuffer, 0);
```

-
-

3. Creating Depth/Stencil Attachment (Optional)

- **Create a Renderbuffer Object:**
- C++

```cpp
unsigned int rbo;
glGenRenderbuffers(1, &rbo);
glBindRenderbuffer(GL_RENDERBUFFER, rbo);
```

glRenderbufferStorage(GL_RENDERBUFFER, GL_DEPTH24_STENCIL8, width, height);

-
-
- **Attach[2] Renderbuffer to FBO:**
- C++

glFramebufferRenderbuffer(GL_FRAMEBUFFER, GL_DEPTH_STENCIL_ATTACHMENT, GL_RENDERBUFFER, rbo);

-
-

4. Check Framebuffer Completeness

- **Ensure the FBO is configured correctly:**
- C++

if (glCheckFramebufferStatus(GL_FRAMEBUFFER) != GL_FRAMEBUFFER_COMPLETE)
{
    std::cout << "ERROR::FRAMEBUFFER:: Framebuffer is not complete!" << std::endl;
}

-
-

5. Rendering to the FBO

- **Bind the FBO:**
- C++

glBindFramebuffer(GL_FRAMEBUFFER, fbo);

-
-
- **Render the scene as usual.**
- **Unbind the FBO:**
- C++

glBindFramebuffer(GL_FRAMEBUFFER, 0);

-
-

6. Using the Rendered Texture

- **Bind the texture to a texture unit:**
- C++

glActiveTexture(GL_TEXTURE0);

glBindTexture(GL_TEXTURE_2D, textureColorBuffer);

-
-
- **Use the texture in a shader for further processing or display.**

Key Considerations:

- **Framebuffer Completeness:** Ensure that the FBO is configured correctly by checking the framebuffer status.
- **Performance:** Creating and using FBOs can have a performance impact, so use them judiciously.
- **Error Handling:** Always check for errors when creating and using FBOs.

6.2 Render-to-Texture (RTT): Rendering to Textures

Render-to-Texture (RTT) is a technique that involves rendering the output of the graphics pipeline to a texture instead of directly to the screen. This allows you to capture the rendered image as a texture, which can then be used for various purposes, such as:

- **Post-processing Effects:**
    - Apply effects like bloom, depth of field, motion blur, and screen-space reflections after the initial rendering pass.
    - Create advanced visual effects by manipulating the rendered image.
- **Shadow Mapping:**
    - Render the scene from the light's perspective to a depth texture.
    - Use this depth texture to determine which parts of the scene are in shadow.
- **Environment Mapping:**
    - Capture the environment around an object using a cube map.
    - Use the captured environment to simulate reflections on the object's surface.
- **Deferred Rendering:**
    - Render scene data (e.g., position, normal, albedo) to separate textures.
    - Perform lighting calculations in a separate pass, using the stored data.

Implementation

1. **Create a Framebuffer Object (FBO):**
   - As described in the previous section, create an FBO and attach a texture as the color attachment.
2. **Bind the FBO:**
   - Bind the FBO before rendering: glBindFramebuffer(GL_FRAMEBUFFER, fbo);
3. **Render the Scene:**
   - Render the scene as usual. The output of the rendering process will be written to the attached texture.
4. **Unbind the FBO:**
   - Unbind the FBO after rendering: glBindFramebuffer(GL_FRAMEBUFFER, 0);
5. **Use the Rendered Texture:**
   - Bind the rendered texture to a texture unit.
   - Use the texture in subsequent rendering passes or for post-processing effects.

Example (Simple RTT for Post-processing):

1. **Render the scene to a texture.**
2. **Bind a new framebuffer.**
3. **Render a full-screen quad.**
4. **In the fragment shader, sample the rendered texture and apply post-processing effects (e.g., a blur filter).**
5. **Display the result to the screen.**

Key Considerations:

- **Performance:** RTT can have a performance impact due to the additional rendering pass.
- **Texture Size:** The size of the render target texture can significantly affect performance and memory usage.

- **Color Format:** Choose an appropriate color format for the render target texture based on the desired output (e.g., RGB, RGBA, HDR).

6.3 Depth and Stencil Buffers: Advanced Rendering Techniques

Depth and Stencil Buffers are essential components of the rendering pipeline, enabling the correct visibility of objects in a 3D scene and supporting advanced rendering techniques.

1. Depth Buffer

- **Purpose:**
    - Determines which fragments are visible based on their depth.
    - Prevents overlapping objects from incorrectly obscuring each other.
- **How it Works:**
    - Stores the depth value of each fragment that has been rendered.
    - When a new fragment is rendered, its depth value is compared to the depth value stored in the buffer.
    - If the new fragment is further away than the existing fragment at that pixel, it is discarded.
- **Enabling Depth Testing:**
- C++

```
glEnable(GL_DEPTH_TEST);
```

-
-

2. Stencil Buffer

- **Purpose:**
  - Provides a bitmask for each pixel.
  - Used for advanced rendering techniques such as:
    - **Stencil Shadows:**
      - Render the shadow from the light source to the stencil buffer.
      - Use the stencil buffer to discard fragments that are in shadow.
    - **Clipping:**
      - Define clipping regions within the scene.
      - Render objects only within the specified regions.
    - **Alpha to Coverage:**
      - Use the alpha value of a fragment to determine how many samples should be covered in multisample anti-aliasing.
- **Stencil Operations:**
  - Stencil tests can be performed on each fragment, and the stencil buffer can be modified based on the test results.
  - Common operations:
    - **Stencil Test:** Compare the stencil value with a reference value.
    - **Stencil Operations:**
      - glStencilOp(GL_KEEP, GL_KEEP, GL_REPLACE):
        - If the stencil test passes, keep the current stencil value.
        - If the stencil test fails, keep the current stencil value.

- If the depth test passes, replace the stencil value with a specified value.

3. Advanced Rendering Techniques

- **Shadow Mapping:**
    - Render the scene from the light's perspective to a depth texture.
    - Use this depth texture to determine which parts of the scene are in shadow.
    - In the main rendering pass, use the stencil buffer to discard fragments that are in shadow.
- **Order-Independent Transparency:**
    - Render transparent objects in a specific order to ensure correct blending.
    - Use the stencil buffer to control the rendering order and prevent incorrect blending.
- **Clipping Planes:**
    - Define clipping planes to restrict rendering to specific regions of the scene.
    - Use the stencil buffer to mask out fragments that fall outside the clipping region.

4. Considerations:

- **Performance:** Stencil operations can have a performance impact, so use them judiciously.
- **Complexity:** Stencil operations can be complex to set up and debug.

Part 3: Real-World Applications

7. 3D Modeling and Scene Graphs

7.1 Loading and Rendering 3D Models

Loading and rendering 3D models is a fundamental task in many OpenGL applications. 3D models are typically represented using file formats such as:

- **.obj:** A simple and widely supported file format.
- **.fbx:** A popular format used in many 3D modeling and animation software.
- **.glTF:** A modern, efficient, and widely adopted file format.

1. Loading 3D Model Data

- **File Parsing:**
  - Read the model file and extract relevant information:
    - **Vertices:** Positions, normals, texture coordinates.
    - **Indices:** Define how vertices are connected to form faces (triangles).
    - **Materials:** Information about materials (colors, textures, etc.).
    - **Hierarchy:** Information about the model's hierarchy (e.g., parent-child relationships between objects).
- **Libraries:**
  - Use libraries like **Assimp** (Open Asset Import Library) to simplify the process of loading and parsing various 3D model file formats.

- Assimp provides functions for loading, processing, and extracting data from 3D models.

2. Creating OpenGL Buffers

- **Create Vertex Buffer Objects (VBOs):**
  - Store vertex data (positions, normals, texture coordinates) in VBOs.
- **Create Element Buffer Objects (EBOs):**
  - Store indices to define the order in which vertices should be drawn.

3. Rendering the Model

- **Bind Buffers:**
  - Bind the VBOs and EBOs to their respective targets.
- **Set Vertex Attributes:**
  - Configure vertex attribute pointers to specify how OpenGL should interpret the vertex data.
- **Draw the Model:**
  - Use glDrawElements() to render the model using the indices stored in the EBO.

4. Handling Materials

- **Load and Bind Textures:**
  - Load textures associated with the model (e.g., diffuse, specular, normal maps).
  - Bind the appropriate textures in the fragment shader.
- **Set Material Properties:**
  - Pass material properties (e.g., ambient, diffuse, specular, shininess) to the shaders.

5. Example (Simplified)

C++

```cpp
// Assuming you have loaded vertex data (vertices), indices,
// and texture coordinates into appropriate buffers

// Bind buffers
glBindBuffer(GL_ARRAY_BUFFER, VBO);
glBindBuffer(GL_ELEMENT_ARRAY_BUFFER, EBO);

// Set vertex attribute pointers
glVertexAttribPointer(0, 3, GL_FLOAT, GL_FALSE, 8 * sizeof(float), (void*)0);
glEnableVertexAttribArray(0);
glVertexAttribPointer(1, 3, GL_FLOAT, GL_FALSE, 8 * sizeof(float), (void*)(3 * sizeof(float)));
glEnableVertexAttribArray(1);
glVertexAttribPointer(2, 2, GL_FLOAT, GL_FALSE, 8 * sizeof(float), (void*)(6 * sizeof(float)));
glEnableVertexAttribArray(2);

// Draw the model
glDrawElements(GL_TRIANGLES, numIndices, GL_UNSIGNED_INT, 0);
```

6. Considerations

- **Performance:** Optimize model loading and rendering for better performance, especially for large and complex models.
- **Memory Management:** Efficiently manage memory to avoid memory leaks and ensure smooth performance.
- **Model Complexity:** Consider simplifying complex models for better performance on less powerful hardware.

7.2 Scene Graphs: Organizing and Managing 3D Scenes

Scene Graphs provide a hierarchical structure for organizing and managing the objects within a 3D scene. This hierarchical representation offers several advantages:

- **Efficient Transformations:** Transformations (translation, rotation, scaling) can be applied to the entire subtree of nodes, reducing the number of matrix calculations.
- **Modularity:** Allows for easier organization and management of complex scenes with many objects.
- **Reusability:** Enables the reuse of entire subtrees of the scene graph.
- **Animation:** Facilitates the creation and management of complex animations.

1. Scene Graph Structure

- **Nodes:**
    - Represent individual objects in the scene (e.g., models, lights, cameras).

- Can contain other nodes as children, forming a hierarchical tree structure.
- **Transformations:**
  - Each node can have associated transformations (translation, rotation, scaling).
  - Transformations are typically applied recursively, starting from the root of the tree.
- **Rendering:**
  - The scene graph is traversed recursively, and the rendering of each node is performed in the correct order.

2. Implementing a Scene Graph

- **Data Structures:**
  - Use data structures like trees (e.g., binary trees, octrees) to represent the hierarchical relationships between nodes.
- **Node Class:**
  - Create a Node class that stores information about the node:
    - **Transformations:** Model matrix, parent node.
    - **Geometry:** Pointers to vertex data, indices, and textures.
    - **Children:** List of child nodes.
- **Rendering Algorithm:**
  - Implement a recursive function to traverse the scene graph and render each node.
  - Calculate the world matrix for each node by combining the node's local transformations with the transformations of its parent nodes.

3. Example (Simplified C++)

C++

```cpp
class Node {
public:
    glm::mat4 modelMatrix;
    std::vector<Node*> children;
    // ... other members (geometry, materials, etc.) ...

    void render() {
        // Calculate world matrix
        // ...

        // Bind buffers, set uniforms, etc.
        // ...

        // Draw geometry
        // ...

        // Render children
        for (Node* child : children) {
            child->render();
```

```
      }
   }
};
```

4. Advanced Techniques

- **Animation:**
    - Animate nodes by modifying their transformations over time.
    - Keyframe animation, skeletal animation, and physics-based animation can be implemented using scene graphs.
- **Culling:**
    - Cull nodes that are not visible to the camera, improving rendering performance.
- **Level of Detail (LOD):**
    - Use the scene graph to manage different levels of detail for objects at varying distances.

7.3 Model Transformation and Animation

Transformations are fundamental for manipulating and animating 3D models in OpenGL. They allow you to:

- **Position objects:** Move objects within the scene.
- **Orient objects:** Rotate objects to face different directions.
- **Scale objects:** Change the size of objects.
- **Create animations:** Smoothly transition between different object states.

1. Transformations

- **Translation:** Shifts the object's position along the x, y, and z axes.
- **Rotation:** Rotates the object around a specific axis.
- **Scaling:** Changes the size of the object along the x, y, and z axes.
- **Matrix Representation:**
  - Transformations are typically represented using 4x4 matrices.
  - Matrix multiplication is used to combine multiple transformations.

2. Model Matrix

- **Purpose:** Represents the transformations applied to the object itself within its local coordinate system.
- **Calculation:**
  - Combine individual transformation matrices (translation, rotation, scaling) in the correct order.
  - The order of matrix multiplication is crucial and affects the final result.
- **Example (C++ with GLM):**
- C++

```
glm::mat4 model = glm::mat4(1.0f); // Identity matrix

model = glm::translate(model, glm::vec3(1.0f, 0.5f, 0.0f)); // Translate

model = glm::rotate(model, glm::radians(45.0f), glm::vec3(0.0f, 1.0f, 0.0f)); // Rotate

model = glm::scale(model, glm::vec3(0.5f, 0.5f, 0.5f)); // Scale
```

-
-

3. Animation

- **Keyframe Animation:**
    - Define keyframes that specify the object's position, rotation, and scale at specific points in time.
    - Interpolate between keyframes to create smooth animation.
- **Skeletal Animation:**
    - Define a skeleton with bones that are connected hierarchically.
    - Animate the skeleton by rotating and translating the bones.
    - Deform the mesh based on the bone transformations.
- **Particle Systems:**
    - Simulate the motion of particles (e.g., smoke, fire, water) using physics and animation techniques.

4. Implementation

- **Update Transformations:**
    - Update the model matrix in each frame of the animation loop.
    - Pass the updated model matrix to the vertex shader.
- **Vertex Shader:**
    - Multiply the vertex positions by the model matrix to apply the transformations.

5. Considerations

- **Performance:**
    - Efficiently calculate and update transformation matrices.

- Optimize animations to minimize the number of calculations.
- **Realism:**
  - Use physically-based animation techniques for more realistic results.

8. Game Development with OpenGL

8.1 Game Loop and Input Handling

A well-structured game loop is essential for creating smooth and responsive gameplay in OpenGL applications.

1. Game Loop

- **Core Structure:**
  - **Initialization:**
    - Initialize OpenGL, create windows, load resources (models, textures, etc.).
  - **Main Loop:**
    - **Input Handling:**
      - Process player input (keyboard, mouse, gamepad).
    - **Update:**
      - Update game logic (e.g., physics, AI, animations).
    - **Render:**
      - Clear the screen, render the scene, and swap buffers.
  - **Cleanup:**
    - Release resources and terminate OpenGL.
- **Example (Simplified C++):**
- C++

while (!glfwWindowShouldClose(window))

```
{
    // Process input
    processInput(window);

    // Update game logic
    deltaTime = glfwGetTime() - lastFrame;
    lastFrame = glfwGetTime();
    // ... update game objects, handle physics, etc. ...

    // Render
    glClearColor(0.2f, 0.3f, 0.3f, 1.0f);
                    glClear(GL_COLOR_BUFFER_BIT  | GL_DEPTH_BUFFER_BIT);
    // ... render the scene ...
    glfwSwapBuffers(window);
}
```

-
-

2. Input Handling

- **Keyboard Input:**
    - Use GLFW functions like glfwGetKey() to detect key presses and releases.

- Handle key combinations (e.g., shift, control) for special actions.
- **Mouse Input:**
    - Use GLFW functions like glfwGetMouseButton() to detect mouse button clicks.
    - Use glfwGetCursorPos() to track mouse movement.
    - Implement mouse look and camera controls.
- **Gamepad Input:**
    - Use GLFW functions to detect gamepad connections and read input from joysticks and buttons.
- **Example (Keyboard Input):**
- C++

if (glfwGetKey(window, GLFW_KEY_ESCAPE) == GLFW_PRESS)

glfwSetWindowShouldClose(window, true);

-
-

3. Considerations

- **Frame Rate Independence:**
    - Use deltaTime to make game logic independent of the frame rate.
    - This ensures consistent behavior regardless of the performance of the user's system.
- **Input Smoothing:**
    - Implement input smoothing techniques to improve responsiveness and prevent jittery movement.
- **User Interface:**
    - Create an intuitive and user-friendly user interface (UI) for interacting with the game.

8.2 Collision Detection and Response

Collision detection and response are crucial aspects of game development, ensuring realistic interactions between objects in the game world.

1. Collision Detection

- **Purpose:** Determine whether two or more objects are intersecting or overlapping.
- **Techniques:**
    - **Bounding Boxes:**
        - Simple and efficient method.
        - Enclose objects within simple shapes (e.g., spheres, cubes) and check for intersections between these bounding shapes.
    - **Ray Casting:**
        - Cast rays from the player or other objects to detect intersections with other objects in the scene.
    - **Spatial Partitioning:**
        - Divide the game world into smaller regions (e.g., grids, octrees).
        - Only check for collisions between objects that reside in the same region.
    - **Physics Engines:**
        - Utilize specialized physics libraries (e.g., Bullet, PhysX) for advanced collision detection and response.

2. Collision Response

- **Purpose:** Determine how objects should behave when a collision occurs.
- **Techniques:**
  - **Impulse-based Response:**
    - Calculate and apply impulses to objects to change their velocities and simulate realistic collisions.
  - **Constraint-based Response:**
    - Use constraints to enforce physical limitations (e.g., prevent objects from penetrating each other).
  - **Game-Specific Logic:**
    - Implement game-specific rules for collision response (e.g., bouncing, sliding, destruction).

3. Implementation

- **Bounding Box Checks:**
  - Calculate the bounding boxes of objects.
  - Check for overlap between bounding boxes.
  - If bounding boxes overlap, perform more precise collision checks.
- **Ray Casting:**
  - Cast rays from the player's position or from the object's movement vector.
  - Check for intersections with other objects using ray-object intersection tests.
- **Physics Engines:**
  - Integrate a physics library into your game.
  - Define object properties (mass, friction, restitution) and simulate physics interactions.

4. Considerations

- **Performance:** Collision detection can be computationally expensive, especially for complex scenes with many objects.
- **Accuracy:** The accuracy of collision detection depends on the chosen techniques and the complexity of the objects involved.
- **Game Design:** Collision detection and response play a crucial role in defining the gameplay experience.

8.3 Character and Object Animation

Animation brings life and dynamism to game worlds. In OpenGL, you can implement various animation techniques to create engaging and realistic motion.

1. Character Animation

- **Skeletal Animation:**
    - A common technique for animating articulated characters (humans, animals).
    - Involves a skeleton with bones connected by joints.
    - Each vertex of the character's mesh is assigned to one or more bones.
    - Bone transformations (rotation, translation) are applied to the vertices to deform the mesh.
    - Libraries like Assimp can help load and process skeletal animation data.
- **Blend Spaces:**
    - Used to transition smoothly between different animations (e.g., walking, running, jumping).
    - Create a grid of animations and blend between them based on the character's speed, direction, and other parameters.

- **Procedural Animation:**
  - Generate animations procedurally using algorithms or physics simulations.
  - Examples: cloth simulation, fluid dynamics, particle effects.

2. Object Animation

- **Keyframe Animation:**
  - Define keyframes that specify the object's position, rotation, and scale at specific points in time.
  - Interpolate between keyframes to create smooth motion.
- **Particle Systems:**
  - Simulate the motion of particles (e.g., smoke, fire, explosions) using forces, velocities, and lifetimes.
- **Physics-Based Animation:**
  - Use physics engines to simulate realistic object motion, such as gravity, collisions, and constraints.

3. Implementation

- **Skeletal Animation:**
  - Load and parse skeletal animation data (bones, joints, animations).
  - Calculate skinning matrices for each vertex, combining bone transformations with skin weights.
  - Pass skinning matrices to the vertex shader.
- **Keyframe Animation:**
  - Interpolate between keyframe data using techniques like linear interpolation or cubic splines.
  - Update object transformations based on the interpolated values.
- **Particle Systems:**

- Generate and update particle positions, velocities, and other properties over time.
- Render particles as points, sprites, or other primitives.

4. Considerations

- **Performance:**
  - Optimize animation calculations to maintain smooth frame rates, especially for complex animations.
  - Utilize hardware acceleration (e.g., GPUs) whenever possible.
- **Realism:**
  - Use physically-based animation techniques and realistic motion capture data to create lifelike animations.

8.4 Game Physics and Dynamics

Game physics and dynamics are crucial for creating realistic and engaging game experiences. They simulate the physical behavior of objects in the game world, such as gravity, collisions, and forces.

1. Core Concepts

- **Rigid Body Dynamics:**
  - Simulates the motion of rigid bodies (objects that do not deform under forces).
  - Involves calculating forces, torques, and accelerations based on Newton's laws of motion.
- **Collision Detection:**
  - Determines whether objects are intersecting or overlapping.

- o Used to calculate collision responses.
- **Constraints:**
  - o Limit the movement of objects, such as joints in a ragdoll character or hinges on a door.

2. Implementation

- **Physics Engines:**
  - o Utilize dedicated physics engines like Bullet, PhysX, or Box2D to handle complex physics simulations.
  - o These libraries provide pre-built implementations of physics algorithms, collision detection, and constraint solvers.
- **Integration with OpenGL:**
  - o Integrate the physics simulation with your OpenGL rendering loop.
  - o Update object positions and orientations based on the results of the physics simulation.

3. Common Physics Simulations

- **Gravity:**
  - o Simulate the effect of gravity on objects, causing them to fall towards the ground.
- **Collisions:**
  - o Simulate collisions between objects, such as bouncing balls, colliding blocks, and character-object interactions.
- **Constraints:**
  - o Simulate constraints such as hinges, joints, and springs to create realistic interactions between objects.
- **Character Movement:**

- Simulate character movement, including walking, jumping, and running, taking into account factors like gravity, friction, and ground collisions.

4. Considerations

- **Performance:**
  - Physics simulations can be computationally expensive, especially for complex scenes with many objects.
  - Optimize physics calculations to maintain smooth frame rates.
- **Accuracy:**
  - Choose appropriate physics parameters and algorithms to achieve realistic and stable simulations.
- **Game Design:**
  - Use physics to enhance gameplay, create challenging puzzles, and add realism to the game world.

9. OpenGL and Other Technologies

9.1 Integrating OpenGL with Other APIs (e.g., DirectX, Vulkan)

While OpenGL remains a powerful and widely-used graphics API, it's sometimes necessary or beneficial to integrate it with other graphics APIs. This can be done for various reasons:

- **Cross-Platform Development:**
    - OpenGL provides a high level of cross-platform compatibility.
    - However, for platform-specific optimizations or access to hardware-specific features, integrating with platform-specific APIs like DirectX (Windows) or Metal (macOS) might be necessary.
- **Performance Optimization:**
    - Some platforms or hardware may offer better performance with specific APIs.
    - Integrating with these APIs can leverage hardware-specific features and optimizations.
- **Feature Access:**
    - Some features might be more readily available or better supported by specific APIs.

Integration Strategies:

- **Abstraction Layers:**
    - Create an abstraction layer that provides a common interface for different graphics APIs.

- This allows you to write platform-independent code while still taking advantage of platform-specific optimizations.
- **Hybrid Rendering:**
  - Utilize different APIs for different rendering tasks.
  - For example, use OpenGL for general rendering and DirectX for specific effects or features.
- **Interoperability:**
  - Some APIs may offer mechanisms for interoperability, allowing you to share resources (e.g., textures, buffers) between different APIs.

Challenges:

- **API Differences:**
  - Significant differences in API design and functionality can make integration challenging.
- **Performance Overhead:**
  - Interoperability mechanisms may introduce performance overhead.
- **Debugging:**
  - Debugging issues that arise from interoperability can be complex.

Examples:

- **OpenGL and DirectX on Windows:**
  - You might use OpenGL for cross-platform compatibility and DirectX for features that are more efficiently implemented on Windows.
- **OpenGL and Vulkan:**
  - Vulkan offers lower-level control and potentially better performance.

- You could use Vulkan for performance-critical rendering tasks and OpenGL for other parts of the application.

Key Considerations:

- **Platform Support:** Carefully consider the target platforms and the availability and performance of different APIs on those platforms.
- **Development Effort:** Assess the additional development effort required for integrating multiple APIs.
- **Performance Testing:** Thoroughly test the performance of your application with different API combinations.

9.2 OpenGL and Virtual Reality (VR)

OpenGL plays a crucial role in the development of immersive Virtual Reality (VR) experiences. It provides the core rendering capabilities to create realistic and interactive virtual environments.

1. Key Considerations for VR Development with OpenGL

- **Stereo Rendering:**
    - VR headsets typically have two displays, one for each eye.
    - OpenGL must render two separate views of the scene, one for each eye, to create the illusion of depth and immersion.
    - This involves calculating and applying appropriate transformations to the view matrix for each eye.
- **Performance:**

- VR applications require high frame rates (typically 90 frames per second or higher) to avoid motion sickness.
- Optimize rendering performance by utilizing techniques like culling, level of detail (LOD), and efficient shaders.

- **Head Tracking:**
    - VR headsets track the user's head movements.
    - Update the view matrix in real-time to reflect the user's head position and orientation.
- **Input Handling:**
    - Handle input from VR controllers (e.g., joysticks, buttons, triggers) to allow users to interact with the virtual environment.
- **Latency:**
    - Minimize latency between user input and visual feedback to prevent motion sickness.

2. Techniques for VR Development

- **Frustum Culling:**
    - Cull objects that are outside the camera's frustum for each eye, improving performance.
- **Multi-View Rendering:**
    - Render both eyes simultaneously using a single draw call, improving performance.
- **Asynchronous Time Warp:**
    - Predict the user's head position and render frames slightly ahead of time to reduce latency.
- **GPU-based Instancing:**
    - Efficiently render multiple instances of the same object using instancing techniques.

3. Example (Simplified Stereo Rendering)

C++

```
// Calculate view matrices for each eye
glm::mat4 leftView = glm::lookAt(leftEyePosition, leftEyeTarget, upVector);
glm::mat4 rightView = glm::lookAt(rightEyePosition, rightEyeTarget, upVector);


// Render the scene for the left eye
glBindFramebuffer(GL_FRAMEBUFFER, leftFbo);
glUniformMatrix4fv(glGetUniformLocation(shaderProgram, "view"), 1, GL_FALSE, glm::value_ptr(leftView));
// ... render the scene ...


// Render the scene for the right eye
glBindFramebuffer(GL_FRAMEBUFFER, rightFbo);
glUniformMatrix4fv(glGetUniformLocation(shaderProgram, "view"), 1, GL_FALSE, glm::value_ptr(rightView));
// ... render the scene ...
```

4. Libraries and Tools

- **VR Frameworks:**
  - Utilize VR frameworks like OpenVR, Oculus SDK, and SteamVR to simplify VR development.

- These frameworks provide tools for handling head tracking, input, and rendering to VR displays.

9.3 OpenGL and Augmented Reality (AR)

OpenGL plays a vital role in the development of Augmented Reality (AR) applications. AR overlays virtual objects onto the real world, and OpenGL provides the core rendering capabilities to create and display these virtual objects.

1. Key Considerations for AR Development with OpenGL

- **Camera Integration:**
  - Integrate with the device's camera to capture the real-world environment.
  - Use camera parameters (e.g., focal length, distortion coefficients) to accurately project virtual objects onto the camera image.
- **Object Tracking:**
  - Track the position and orientation of the device (e.g., using computer vision techniques like ARKit or ARCore) to accurately place virtual objects in the real world.
- **Scene Understanding:**
  - Understand the real-world environment (e.g., detect planes, surfaces, and objects) to intelligently place and anchor virtual objects.
- **Occlusion Handling:**
  - Accurately occlude virtual objects by real-world objects (e.g., a virtual object should be hidden behind a real-world object).
- **Performance:**

- Ensure real-time rendering performance to maintain a smooth and responsive AR experience.

2. Techniques for AR Development

- **Marker-Based AR:**
  - Use visual markers (e.g., QR codes) to track the position and orientation of the device.
  - Overlay virtual objects on or around the detected markers.
- **Markerless AR:**
  - Track the device's position and orientation using computer vision techniques like Simultaneous Localization and Mapping (SLAM).
  - Allows for more natural and seamless integration of virtual objects into the real world.
- **Object Recognition and Tracking:**
  - Detect and track real-world objects (e.g., faces, objects) using computer vision algorithms.
  - Overlay virtual objects on or around the recognized objects.

3. Example (Simplified AR Application)

1. **Capture the camera image:**
   - Obtain the camera image from the device.
2. **Process the image:**
   - Detect and track features in the image using computer vision techniques.
3. **Calculate camera pose:**
   - Determine the position and orientation of the camera in the real world.
4. **Render virtual objects:**

- Use OpenGL to render virtual objects, applying the appropriate transformations based on the camera pose.
5. **Overlay virtual objects:**
   - Combine the rendered virtual objects with the camera image to create the augmented reality view.

4. Libraries and Tools

- **AR Frameworks:**
  - Utilize AR frameworks like ARKit (iOS), ARCore (Android), and Vuforia to simplify AR development.
  - These frameworks provide tools for camera access, object tracking, and scene understanding.

Part 4: Best Practices and Optimization

10. OpenGL Debugging and Profiling

10.1 Debugging Techniques: Using OpenGL's Debug Output

Debugging OpenGL applications can be challenging due to the complexity of the graphics pipeline and the potential for subtle errors. OpenGL provides a powerful debugging mechanism through its debug output functionality.

1. Enabling Debug Output

- **Create a Debug Context:**
    - When creating the OpenGL context, enable the debug context flag:
    - C++

glfwWindowHint(GLFW_OPENGL_DEBUG_CONTEXT, GL_TRUE);

    -
    -

- **Set the Debug Output Callback:**
    - Register a callback function that will be called by OpenGL whenever a debug message is generated:
    - C++

void GLAPIENTRY DebugOutput(GLenum source,

GLenum type,

```c
                        unsigned int id,
                        GLenum severity,
                        int length,
                        const char* message,
                        const void* userParam)
{
    // Print or log the debug message
    fprintf(stderr, "GL CALLBACK: %s type = 0x%x, severity = 0x%x, message = %s\n",
            (type == GL_DEBUG_TYPE_ERROR ? "** GL ERROR **" :
             (type == GL_DEBUG_TYPE_DEPRECATED_BEHAVIOR ? "** DEPRECATED BEHAVIOR **" :
              (type == GL_DEBUG_TYPE_UNDEFINED_BEHAVIOR ? "** UNDEFINED BEHAVIOR **" :
               (type == GL_DEBUG_TYPE_PORTABILITY ? "** PORTABILITY **" :
                (type == GL_DEBUG_TYPE_PERFORMANCE ? "** PERFORMANCE **" :
                 (type == GL_DEBUG_TYPE_MARKER ? "** MARKER **" :
                  (type == GL_DEBUG_TYPE_PUSH_GROUP ? "** PUSH_GROUP **" :
```

```
                    (type == GL_DEBUG_TYPE_POP_GROUP ? "**
POP_GROUP **" :
                "** UNKNOWN **")))))),
        type, severity, message);
}


glEnable(GL_DEBUG_OUTPUT);

glEnable(GL_DEBUG_OUTPUT_SYNCHRONOUS);

glDebugMessageCallback(DebugOutput, nullptr);
```
-
  -

2. Filtering Debug Messages

- **Severity Levels:**
  - Control the types of messages that are displayed:
    - GL_DEBUG_SEVERITY_HIGH
    - GL_DEBUG_SEVERITY_MEDIUM
    - GL_DEBUG_SEVERITY_LOW
    - GL_DEBUG_SEVERITY_NOTIFICATION
- **Source Types:**
  - Filter messages based on their source (e.g., API, application, window system).
- **Message IDs:**
  - Filter messages based on their unique IDs.
- **Example:**
- C++

```
glDebugMessageControl(GL_DONT_CARE,
```

GL_DONT_CARE,

GL_DONT_CARE,

0,

NULL,

GL_FALSE); // Disable all messages

glDebugMessageControl(GL_DONT_CARE,

GL_DONT_CARE,

GL_DEBUG_SEVERITY_HIGH,

0,

NULL,

GL_TRUE); // Enable only high-severity messages

-
-

3. Using Debug Output for Error Detection

- **Identify OpenGL Errors:**
    - Detect and address issues like invalid function calls, invalid state changes, and resource leaks.
- **Track Shader Compilation Errors:**
    - Identify and fix errors in your vertex and fragment shaders.
- **Find Performance Bottlenecks:**
    - Analyze performance-related messages to identify areas for optimization.

4. Considerations

- **Performance Overhead:**

- Enabling debug output can have a slight performance impact.
- **Message Filtering:**
  - Effectively filter debug messages to avoid being overwhelmed by information.

10.2 Profiling Performance: Identifying Bottlenecks

Profiling is crucial for identifying performance bottlenecks in your OpenGL applications. It helps you pinpoint areas that are consuming the most resources (CPU or GPU) and guide optimization efforts.

1. Profiling Tools

- **Integrated Development Environments (IDEs):**
  - Many IDEs (like Visual Studio, CLion) have built-in profiling tools that can track CPU usage, memory allocation, and function call times.
- **Graphics Debugging Tools:**
  - Tools like NVIDIA Nsight Systems, AMD Radeon Profiler, and Intel GPA provide detailed insights into GPU performance.
  - They can capture performance metrics like frame times, GPU utilization, and shader execution times.
- **OpenGL Performance Counters:**
  - OpenGL provides performance counters that can be queried to gather information about GPU activity, such as vertex processing rate, pixel fill rate, and memory bandwidth.

2. Identifying Performance Bottlenecks

- **Frame Rate Analysis:**
    - Monitor the frame rate and identify any significant drops or inconsistencies.
- **CPU Profiling:**
    - Identify CPU-bound tasks, such as complex calculations, physics simulations, and input handling.
- **GPU Profiling:**
    - Analyze GPU usage, identify shader bottlenecks, and pinpoint areas where the GPU is underutilized.
- **Memory Usage:**
    - Monitor memory usage to identify potential memory leaks or excessive memory consumption.
- **Draw Calls:**
    - Minimize the number of draw calls to reduce overhead.
    - Combine multiple draw calls into a single draw call whenever possible.
- **Overdraw:**
    - Identify and reduce overdraw, where pixels are rendered multiple times unnecessarily.

3. Optimization Techniques

- **Reduce Overdraw:**
    - Use depth testing and backface culling to discard invisible fragments.
    - Optimize scene geometry and reduce the number of polygons.
- **Improve Shader Performance:**
    - Optimize shader code for efficiency, minimize branching, and utilize hardware-specific features.
- **Minimize State Changes:**

- Minimize the number of state changes (e.g., binding textures, setting uniforms) by grouping objects with similar properties.
- **Utilize Hardware Features:**
  - Take advantage of hardware features like instancing, tessellation, and geometry shaders to improve performance.
- **Optimize Data Structures:**
  - Use efficient data structures (e.g., octrees, k-d trees) to accelerate spatial queries and collision detection.

4. Considerations

- **Profiling Overhead:**
  - Profiling tools can introduce overhead, so use them judiciously.
- **Platform-Specific Considerations:**
  - Profiling techniques and tools may vary depending on the platform and hardware.

10.3 Optimization Strategies: Reducing Overdraw and Improving Efficiency

Optimizing OpenGL applications is crucial for achieving smooth frame rates and a responsive user experience. Here are key strategies to reduce overdraw and improve overall efficiency:

1. Reducing Overdraw

- **Overdraw:** Occurs when pixels are rendered multiple times, even though they are fully or partially obscured by other objects. This wastes GPU resources.
- **Techniques:**

- **Depth Testing:** Enables the depth buffer to discard fragments that are further away than previously rendered fragments at the same pixel.
- **Backface Culling:** Discards polygons that face away from the camera, as they are not visible.
- **Early Z-Culling:** Perform depth tests as early as possible in the pipeline to discard invisible fragments quickly.
- **Occlusion Culling:**
  - Identify objects that are completely occluded by other objects and avoid rendering them entirely.
  - Techniques like hardware occlusion queries and software-based occlusion culling can be used.
- **View Frustum Culling:**
  - Discard objects that are outside the camera's viewing frustum (the pyramid-shaped region that the camera can see).

2. Improving Shader Efficiency

- **Minimize Instructions:**
  - Reduce the number of instructions in your shaders as much as possible.
  - Use built-in functions and hardware-specific features whenever possible.
- **Data Reuse:**
  - Reuse calculated values whenever possible to avoid redundant calculations.
- **Branching:**
  - Minimize the use of conditional statements (if/else) within shaders, as they can impact performance.
- **Precision:**

- Use appropriate data types (e.g., float, mediump float) to avoid unnecessary precision.

3. Batching Draw Calls

- **Reduce the number of draw calls:**
  - Combine multiple draw calls into a single draw call whenever possible.
  - Group objects with similar rendering states (e.g., materials, textures) together.
  - Utilize instancing to render multiple instances of the same object with different transformations in a single draw call.

4. Optimizing Data Structures

- **Efficient Data Storage:**
  - Use efficient data structures (e.g., vertex buffer objects, index buffers) to store and access vertex data.
  - Minimize data transfers between CPU and GPU.
- **Spatial Partitioning:**
  - Use spatial partitioning techniques (e.g., octrees, k-d trees) to organize objects in the scene, making it easier to perform visibility checks and collision detection.

5. Utilizing Hardware Features

- **Tessellation:**
  - Use tessellation shaders to dynamically adjust the level of detail of objects based on distance and view direction.
- **Geometry Shaders:**
  - Utilize geometry shaders for tasks like instancing, culling, and generating complex geometry.
- **Compute Shaders:**

- Offload computationally intensive tasks (e.g., physics simulations, AI) to the GPU.

11. Cross-Platform Development with OpenGL

OpenGL is designed to be a cross-platform API, allowing developers to write graphics applications that can run on various operating systems with minimal modifications. However, there are platform-specific considerations and implementations that need to be addressed for successful cross-platform development.

1. Core Concepts

- **Platform Abstraction:** OpenGL itself defines a standard interface for graphics rendering.
- **Platform-Specific Implementations:**
    - **Windows:** Uses the WGL (Windows Graphics Library) for creating OpenGL contexts and managing windows.
    - **macOS:** Uses the CGL (Core Graphics Layer) for OpenGL interactions.
    - **Linux:** Uses the GLX (OpenGL Extension to the X Window System) for creating and managing OpenGL contexts.
- **Cross-Platform Libraries:**
    - Libraries like GLFW (Graphics Library Framework) and SDL (Simple DirectMedia Layer) provide a cross-platform abstraction layer, simplifying window creation, input handling, and OpenGL context management.

2. Key Considerations

- **Window System Integration:**
  - Handle window creation, input events (keyboard, mouse), and event loops differently on each platform.
  - Utilize cross-platform libraries like GLFW or SDL to abstract away platform-specific windowing details.
- **Context Creation:**
  - Create OpenGL contexts using the appropriate platform-specific functions (WGL, CGL, GLX).
  - Ensure proper context creation and initialization on each platform.
- **Extension Loading:**
  - Load OpenGL extensions using platform-specific mechanisms (e.g., wglGetProcAddress on Windows, glXGetProcAddress on Linux).
  - Libraries like GLAD or GLEW can simplify extension loading across platforms.
- **Platform-Specific Features:**
  - Be mindful of platform-specific features that may not be available on all platforms.
  - Use conditional compilation or platform-specific code blocks to handle such cases.
- **Build Systems:**
  - Use build systems like CMake to manage platform-specific build configurations, libraries, and include paths.

3. Example (Simplified Window Creation with GLFW)

C++

```cpp
#include <GLFW/glfw3.h>
```

```cpp
int main() {
    // Initialize GLFW
    if (!glfwInit())
        return -1;


    // Create a window (platform-specific implementation handled by GLFW)
    GLFWwindow* window = glfwCreateWindow(800, 600, "My OpenGL Window", NULL, NULL);
    if (window == NULL) {
        glfwTerminate();
        return -1;
    }


    // ... (rest of the OpenGL initialization) ...

    glfwTerminate();
    return 0;
}
```

4. Best Practices

- **Use cross-platform libraries:**
    - Leverage libraries like GLFW, SDL, and Assimp to minimize platform-specific code.
- **Test thoroughly:**
    - Test your application on all target platforms to ensure proper functionality and performance.
- **Keep platform-specific code to a minimum:**
    - Isolate platform-specific code in separate files or modules to improve code maintainability.

Cross-Platform Development Frameworks for OpenGL

Cross-platform frameworks simplify OpenGL development by abstracting away many of the platform-specific details, allowing developers to write code that can run on Windows, macOS, Linux, and potentially other operating systems with minimal modifications.

1. GLFW (Graphics Library Framework)

- **Focus:** Primarily focused on window creation, input handling, and OpenGL context management.
- **Strengths:**
    - Simple to use and easy to integrate.
    - Cross-platform support for Windows, macOS, Linux, and other platforms.
    - Active community and well-maintained.
- **Limitations:**
    - Primarily focused on core windowing and input handling.
    - Offers limited functionality beyond OpenGL.

2. SDL (Simple DirectMedia Layer)

- **Focus:** A broader-scope library providing support for windowing, input, audio, image loading, and more.
- **Strengths:**
    - Highly versatile and feature-rich.
    - Supports a wide range of multimedia functionalities.
    - Large and active community.
- **Limitations:**
    - Can be more complex to use than GLFW for simpler projects.

3. Qt

- **Focus:** A comprehensive framework for creating cross-platform applications with a rich set of UI components and tools.
- **Strengths:**
    - Provides a high-level abstraction for user interface development.
    - Supports OpenGL integration.
    - Excellent for creating complex and feature-rich applications.
- **Limitations:**
    - Can have a steeper learning curve due to its broader scope.

4. Considerations When Choosing a Framework

- **Project Scope:**
    - For simple OpenGL projects, GLFW might be sufficient.
    - For more complex applications with multimedia needs, SDL or Qt might be more suitable.
- **Features:**

- Evaluate the specific features offered by each framework and choose the one that best aligns with your project requirements.
- **Community and Support:**
  - Consider the size and activity of the community and the availability of support resources.

5. Example (Window Creation with GLFW)

C++

```cpp
#include <GLFW/glfw3.h>

int main() {
  if (!glfwInit())
    return -1;

  // Create a window (GLFW handles platform-specific creation)
  GLFWwindow* window = glfwCreateWindow(800, 600, "My OpenGL Window", NULL, NULL);
  if (window == NULL) {
    glfwTerminate();
    return -1;
  }
```

```
// ... (rest of OpenGL initialization) ...

    glfwTerminate();

    return 0;

}
```

By effectively utilizing cross-platform frameworks, you can significantly streamline the development process, improve code maintainability, and ensure that your OpenGL applications run smoothly across various operating systems.

Fdfjjhhh

BB

12. The Future of OpenGL: Latest Versions and Extensions

12.1 Latest OpenGL Versions and Extensions

OpenGL continues to evolve with new versions and extensions, offering enhanced capabilities and improved performance.

1. Latest OpenGL Versions

- **OpenGL 4.6:** The latest major version, released in 2017, introduces features like:
    - **Compute Shader Enhancements:** Improved support for general-purpose computing on the GPU.
    - **Tessellation Enhancements:** Enhanced tessellation control and evaluation shaders.
    - **New Primitive Types:** Support for new primitive types, including lines with adjacency and quads.
    - **Improved Debug Capabilities:** Enhanced debugging features for better error detection and performance analysis.
- **OpenGL ES 3.2:** The latest version of OpenGL ES (for embedded systems) focuses on:
    - **Performance Enhancements:** Optimized rendering pipelines and improved support for mobile and embedded devices.
    - **Compute Shader Support:** Enhanced support for compute shaders on embedded platforms.

- **Support for Modern Features:** Continued support for modern OpenGL features, such as shaders, textures, and framebuffers.

2. Key Extensions

- **ARB_compute_shader:** Enables general-purpose computing on the GPU using compute shaders.
- **ARB_tessellation_shader:** Provides support for tessellation control and evaluation shaders.
- **EXT_texture_compression_s3tc:** Supports S3TC (S3 Texture Compression) for efficient texture compression.
- **ARB_framebuffer_object:** Enables the creation of custom framebuffers for advanced rendering techniques.

3. Future Directions

- **Continued Performance Improvements:** Ongoing efforts to improve rendering performance and efficiency, especially on modern GPUs.
- **Ray Tracing Support:** While not directly part of the core OpenGL specification, ray tracing extensions and libraries are available for implementing advanced rendering techniques like ray tracing and path tracing.
- **Cross-Platform Compatibility:** Continued emphasis on maintaining cross-platform compatibility across different operating systems and hardware platforms.
- **Integration with Other APIs:** Exploring interoperability with other graphics APIs like Vulkan and DirectX.

4. Key Considerations

- **Hardware Support:**
    - Not all GPUs support the latest OpenGL versions and extensions.

- It's crucial to check for hardware compatibility before using advanced features.
- **Driver Support:**
  - Ensure that you have the latest graphics drivers installed for optimal performance and compatibility.

5. Conclusion

OpenGL continues to evolve with new features and extensions, providing developers with powerful tools for creating visually stunning and high-performance graphics applications. By staying informed about the latest versions and extensions, you can leverage the full potential of OpenGL and create cutting-edge graphics experiences.

12.2 Trends in Real-Time 3D Graphics

Real-time 3D graphics continue to evolve rapidly, driven by advancements in hardware, software, and algorithmic techniques. Here are some of the key trends shaping the future of this field:

1. Ray Tracing

- **Realism:** Ray tracing simulates the physical behavior of light, resulting in stunningly realistic visuals with accurate reflections, refractions, shadows, and global illumination.
- **Hardware Acceleration:** Dedicated ray tracing hardware (like NVIDIA RTX and AMD RDNA 2) has significantly accelerated ray tracing performance, making it more accessible for real-time applications.
- **Applications:** Ray tracing is increasingly used in games, film, and other industries to achieve photorealistic visuals.

2. Artificial Intelligence (AI) and Machine Learning (ML)

- **AI-Powered Graphics:** AI is being used to generate 3D models, textures, and animations, automate tasks, and improve rendering performance.
- **Neural Networks:** Neural networks are used for tasks such as image super-resolution, style transfer, and generating realistic textures and materials.
- **AI-Driven Character Animation:** AI techniques are used to create more lifelike and believable character animations.

3. Virtual Reality (VR) and Augmented Reality (AR)

- **Immersive Experiences:** VR and AR continue to push the boundaries of real-time 3D graphics, demanding high frame rates, low latency, and realistic rendering.
- **Hardware Advancements:** Continued advancements in VR/AR hardware, such as head-mounted displays and tracking technologies, are driving the development of more immersive and interactive experiences.

4. Cloud Gaming and Streaming

- **Cloud-Based Rendering:**
  - Cloud gaming services allow users to stream high-fidelity 3D graphics from powerful servers to their devices.
  - This enables access to demanding graphics experiences on a wider range of devices.

5. Metaverse and Spatial Computing

- **Evolving Technologies:** The metaverse and spatial computing are emerging fields that will heavily rely on advanced 3D graphics technologies.
- **New Challenges and Opportunities:** These technologies present new challenges and opportunities for real-time 3D

graphics, such as the need for highly realistic and interactive virtual environments.

6. Ethical Considerations

- **Responsible AI:**
    - Ensuring that AI-powered graphics technologies are used responsibly and ethically.
    - Addressing potential biases and ensuring fairness and transparency.
- **Environmental Impact:**
    - Minimizing the environmental impact of 3D graphics technologies through energy-efficient hardware and software.

Key Takeaways:

- Real-time 3D graphics is a rapidly evolving field with exciting advancements in areas like ray tracing, AI, and VR/AR.
- These advancements are pushing the boundaries of what's possible in terms of visual quality, realism, and interactivity.
- Ethical considerations are crucial as these technologies continue to evolve and impact our lives.

Appendix

A: OpenGL Mathematics

1. Vectors

- **Definition:** A vector represents a quantity with both magnitude and direction.
- **Representation:** In 3D graphics, vectors are typically represented as 3-dimensional arrays: [x, y, z].
- **Operations:**
    - **Addition:** v1 + v2 = [v1.x + v2.x, v1.y + v2.y, v1.z + v2.z]
    - **Subtraction:** v1 - v2 = [v1.x - v2.x, v1.y - v2.y, v1.z - v2.z]
    - **Scalar Multiplication:** k * v = [k * v.x, k * v.y, k * v.z]
    - **Dot Product:**
        - v1 · v2 = v1.x * v2.x + v1.y * v2.y + v1.z * v2.z
        - Used to calculate the angle between two vectors.
    - **Cross Product:**
        - v1 x v2 results in a vector perpendicular to both v1 and v2.
        - Used to calculate surface normals.
    - **Normalization:**
        - Scales a vector to unit length (magnitude of 1).

2. Matrices

- **Definition:** A 2D array of numbers arranged in rows and columns.
- **In 3D Graphics:** Used to represent transformations (translation, rotation, scaling), projections, and other operations on vectors.
- **Matrix Multiplication:**
  - Used to combine transformations and apply them to vectors.
  - Matrix multiplication is not commutative (order matters).

3. Quaternions

- **Definition:**
  - An extension of complex numbers, representing rotation in 3D space.
  - More efficient and less prone to gimbal lock than Euler angles.
- **Representation:**
  - Typically represented as [w, x, y, z], where w is the scalar part and [x, y, z] is the vector part.
- **Advantages:**
  - Efficient representation and interpolation of rotations.
  - Avoids gimbal lock, a problem that can occur when using Euler angles.

4. Libraries

- **GLM (OpenGL Mathematics):** A popular open-source library that provides a comprehensive set of mathematical functions for OpenGL, including vector, matrix, and quaternion operations.

5. Importance in OpenGL

- **Transformations:** Matrices are used extensively in OpenGL to transform vertices, model objects, and define camera views.
- **Lighting:** Vector operations are crucial for calculating lighting and shading effects (e.g., diffuse, specular).
- **Animations:** Quaternions are often used for smooth and efficient character and object animations.

6. Conclusion

A solid understanding of vectors, matrices, and quaternions is essential for effective 3D graphics programming with OpenGL. These mathematical concepts form the foundation for many of the core operations involved in rendering 3D scenes.

B: GLSL Syntax and Built-in Functions

1. Introduction

GLSL (OpenGL Shading Language) is a high-level shading language used to program the vertex and fragment shaders within the OpenGL pipeline. It's a C-like language with its own set of data types, functions, and keywords specifically designed for graphics programming.

2. Basic Syntax

- **Data Types:**
  - **Scalars:** float, int, bool
  - **Vectors:** vec2, vec3, vec4 (represent 2D, 3D, and 4D vectors)
  - **Matrices:** mat2, mat3, mat4
  - **Other:** sampler2D, sampler3D, samplerCube (for textures)

- **Variables:** Declared with their data type:
    - float myFloat;
    - vec3 myVector;
    - mat4 myMatrix;
- **Variables:** Can be declared as uniform (values set from the CPU) or in/out (for input/output variables between shader stages).
- **Operators:**
    - Arithmetic operators: +, -, *, /
    - Comparison operators: ==, !=, >, <, >=, <=
    - Logical operators: &&, ||, !
    - Vector and matrix operations: * (multiplication), +, -
- **Control Flow:**
    - if, else, if...else if...else
    - for, while loops
- **Functions:**
    - Can define custom functions within shaders.
    - Built-in functions for common mathematical operations (see below).

3. Built-in Functions

GLSL provides a rich set of built-in functions for various mathematical operations, including:

- **Vector Operations:**
    - length(): Calculate the length of a vector.
    - normalize(): Normalize a vector to unit length.
    - dot(): Calculate the dot product of two vectors.
    - cross(): Calculate the cross product of two vectors.
    - distance(): Calculate the distance between two points.
- **Matrix Operations:**
    - transpose(): Transpose a matrix.
    - inverse(): Calculate the inverse of a matrix.

- - determinant(): Calculate the determinant of a matrix.
- **Trigonometric Functions:**
  - sin(), cos(), tan(), asin(), acos(), atan(), atan2()
- **Texture Sampling:**
  - texture(): Sample a texture at given coordinates.
- **Color Manipulation:**
  - mix(): Linearly interpolate between two colors.
- **Noise Functions:**
  - noise(), fractNoise() (for generating noise patterns)

4. Example

OpenGL Shading Language

```glsl
#version 330 core

layout (location = 0) in vec3 aPos;

void main()
{
    gl_Position = vec4(aPos, 1.0);
}
```

This is a simple vertex shader that simply passes the input vertex position to the next stage in the pipeline.

5. Key Considerations

- **Precision:** GLSL supports different precision qualifiers (e.g., highp, mediump, lowp) to control the precision of floating-point calculations.
- **Hardware Support:** The availability and performance of certain features may vary depending on the GPU.

www.ingramcontent.com/pod-product-compliance
Lightning Source LLC
Chambersburg PA
CBHW062107220526
45471CB00010B/3636